"*Poetry and Psychoanalysis: The Openin* open our field. It opens our capacity to use our imagination in our work, indeed our lives, as psychotherapists. Poetry is the key to that opening. In Shaddock's hand the poetry is not 'applied' to therapy, rather it inspires."

– Malcolm Owen Slavin, Ph.D., author of forthcoming
*Original Loss: Grieving Existential Trauma in Art
and the Art of Psychoanalysis*

"I wouldn't have imagined I could read a book that would teach me something new both about psychoanalysis (especially about how the analyst listens) and about poets I have lived with for decades, Dante, Blake. Everyone interested in either poetry or psychoanalysis should read this book."

– Alan Williamson, Warren Wilson College, author
of *Franciscan Notes* and *Almost a Girl: Male
Writers and Female Identification*

"In *Poetry and Psychoanalysis: The Opening of the Field*, David Shaddock reveals the unexpected kinship between clinical psychoanalysis and the art of poetry. In both, a speaker (poet or patient) speaks intimately to an other (therapist or reader) the deepest experiences of the heart. In both, meaning is carried in sounds, rhythms, memories and dreams. In both, expression is the medium of transformation. In this marvelous book, Shaddock, poet and psychoanalyst, reveals how such transformation comes to be."

– Jeffrey Stern, Ph.D., literary critic, Training and Supervising
Analyst, Chicago Psychoanalytic Institute

Poetry and Psychoanalysis

Poetry and Psychoanalysis: The Opening of the Field provides a guide to applying a poet's imagination and precision of language to the healing endeavors of psychoanalysis while making a lucid journey through 2,000 years of transformative poetry from Virgil, Dante and Blake to the contemporary poet Claudia Rankine.

Patients enter treatment with the hope of being recognized and the hope for transformation of a painful experience. David Shaddock shows how poetry can guide psychoanalysts towards meeting that hope. The book is based on the proposition that an accurate recognition of what is leads to the opening of what could be. The imaginative space that opens between poem and reader or therapist and patient can be a place of healing and transformation.

Poetry and Psychoanalysis will appeal to psychoanalysts and psychoanalytic psychotherapists interested in using literature and creativity as inspiration for both their clinical work and personal growth, as well as all who love poetry.

David Shaddock, Ph.D., is an award-winning poet and psychotherapist. He is author of four books of poetry and two on couples therapy. His play *In a Company of Seekers* was performed at the 2012 Spoleto Arts Festival in Italy. He co-leads the couples therapy interest group for the International Association for Psychoanalytic Self Psychology.

Art, Creativity, and Psychoanalysis book series
George Hagman, LSCW
Series Editor

The *Art, Creativity, and Psychoanalysis* book series seeks to highlight original, cutting-edge studies of the relationship between psychoanalysis and the world of art and the psychology of artists, with subject matter including the psychobiography of artists, the creative process, the psychology of aesthetic experience, as well as the aesthetic, creative and artistic aspects of psychoanalysis and psychoanalytic psychotherapy. *Art, Creativity, and Psychoanalysis* promotes a vision of psychoanalysis as a creative art, the clinical effectiveness of which can be enhanced when we better understand and utilize artistic and creative processes at its core.

The series welcomes proposals from psychoanalytic therapists from all professional groups and theoretical models, as well as artists, art historians and art critics informed by a psychoanalytic perspective. For a full list of all titles in the series, please visit the Routledge website at: www.routledge.com/ACAPBS.

Poetry and Psychoanalysis

The Opening of the Field

David Shaddock

Routledge
Taylor & Francis Group

LONDON AND NEW YORK

First published 2020
by Routledge
2 Park Square, Milton Park, Abingdon, Oxon OX14 4RN

and by Routledge
52 Vanderbilt Avenue, New York, NY 10017

Routledge is an imprint of the Taylor & Francis Group, an informa business

British Library Cataloguing-in-Publication Data
A catalogue record for this book is available from the British Library

Library of Congress Cataloging-in-Publication Data
A catalog record for this book has been requested

ISBN: 978-0-415-69900-6 (hbk)
ISBN: 978-0-415-69901-3 (pbk)
ISBN: 978-0-429-28922-4 (ebk)

Typeset in Times New Roman
by Apex CoVantage, LLC

Often I am permitted to return to a meadow as if it were a given property
of the mind that certain properties hold against chaos.

> Robert Duncan, "Often I Am Permitted
> to Return to a Meadow" (1960)

Contents

Acknowledgments

I would like to first acknowledge George Hagman, whose tireless commitment to the integration of psychoanalysis and the arts underlies this project both spiritually and physically. George formed a group of analyst/artists years ago that I was fortunate enough to be part of. We presented at conferences and festivals internationally and across the U.S., and many of the thoughts that grew out of that collaboration found their way into this book. Further, George suggested I write this book and helped facilitate its publication.

I want to express a note of deepest gratitude to Cindy Hyden, my friend and the editor of all three of my nonfiction books, for her generous reading and suggestions. It is one of life's greatest pleasures to feel seen and understood. A special shout-out is in order to Sophie Kline and Brad Kline for editorial assistance and to Florence Faizi for her generous help with the references. Thanks to Charles Bath, Alec Selwyn and Kate Hawes at Routledge, Ganesh Pawan Kumar Agoor at Apex CoVantage for seeing this project through.

Much of the thinking about poetry that went into this book grew out of my poetry study group, which has been going strong for over 20 years, so thanks to Sandra Gilbert, Dan Belm, Mary Mackey, Lucy Phoenix, Donna Brookman, Murray Silverstein, Marsha Silverstein, Anita Barrows, Dawn McGuire and Peter Dale Scott. Anita, Dawn and Peter also were gracious enough to read and comment on individual chapters. And, as always, thanks to my wife, Toby, for support and encouragement.

Finally, grateful acknowledgment is made to the following publishers for permission to cite their published works:

A version of Chapter 1 was first published in *Psychoanalytic Inquiry*, Volume 26, 2006 – Issue 3. Used by permission.

A version of Chapter 2 was first published in *Art, Creativity and Psychoanalysis: Perspectives from Analyst-Artists*. George Hagman, editor. Copyright 2016, Routledge. Used by permission.

A version of Chapter 4 was published in *Psychoanalysis Self and Context*, Volume 15, Issue 1, pp. 100–105. Used by permission.

A version of Chapter 9 was published in *Psychoanalysis Self and Context*, Volume 14, Issue 3, pp. 323–333. Used by permission.

Grateful acknowledgment is made for permission to quote the following:

Excerpt from "Questo Muro" from *We Are the Hunger* by Anita Barrows. Copyright © 2017 by Anita Barrows. Reprinted with the permission of the author.

Excerpt from "Eating Babies" from *Swimming in the Rain* by Chana Bloch. Copyright © 2015 by Chana Bloch. Reprinted with the permission of The Permissions Company, Inc., on behalf of Autumn House Press, www.autumnhouse.org.

Excerpt from "Before Spring" from *New Collected Poems* by Eavan Boland. Copyright © 2008 by Eavan Boland. Used by permission of W.W. Norton & Company, Inc., and Carcanet Press, Ltd.

Excerpt from "When I heard you were dead, Heraclitus" by Callimachus, translated by Edmund Keeley, in *The Greek Poets*, edited by Peter Constantine et al. (New York: W.W. Norton & Company, 2010). Reprinted with the permission of the translator.

Excerpt from "Dream-Driven on the cir-" from *Last Poems* by Paul Celan, translated by Katharine Washburn and Margret Guillemin. Copyright © 1986 by Katharine Washburn and Margret Guillemin. Reprinted by permission of Suhrkamp Verlag.

Excerpt from *Inferno* by Dante, translated by Michael Parma. Copyright © 2002 by Michael Parma. Used by permission of W.W. Norton & Company, Inc. Excerpts from *Purgatorio*, translated by W.S. Merwin. Copyright © 2000 by W.S. Merwin. Reprinted by permission of The Permissions Company, Inc., on behalf of Copper Canyon Press, www.coppercanyonpress.org, and the Wiley Agency, LLC.

Excerpts from "There's a certain Slant of light" and "I felt a Funeral, in my Brain" from *The Poems of Emily Dickinson*, edited by Thomas H. Johnson, The Belknap Press of Harvard University Press, Copyright 1951,

Preface

This book is based on the proposition that an accurate recognition of what is leads to the opening of what could be. "You have to stay so armored just to get through your day," a therapist tells her lesbian client, "it's hard to come home and open up to intimacy." "There is a certain Slant of light/ Winter afternoons/That oppresses," writes Emily Dickinson.

The field that opens when the real is noted has different names in different universes of discourse. Czeslaw Milosz calls it a second space; contemporary psychoanalysis often refers to it as the third; poets at least since the Romantics call it the imagination. It is almost but not quite coextensive with heaven in religious discourse. As we see in the Divine *Commedia* of Dante, it is a process, a dialogue (or series of dialogues), a notation of woes, a journey to love. The field is, in the language of chaos theory, *emergent*. It has never existed before, though the possibility of recompense it offers may seem familiar. It is as near as a deep breath, as exotic as a series of waking dreams or visions. "So much/depends upon//a red wheel/ barrow," writes William Carlos Williams (1991a, p. 224). "When the sun rises, do you not see a round disc of fire somewhat like a guinea? Oh! no, no! I see an innumerable company of the heavenly host crying 'Holy, holy, holy is the Lord God Almighty!'" writes William Blake (1970, p. 555).

It is also, always, dialogic. Obviously in psychotherapy, less obviously in poetry, where the reader remains an imagined other. Walt Whitman writes: "This hour I tell things in confidence/I might not tell everybody but I will tell you" (1983, p. 43). The mutuality that emerges from a moment of shared perception constellates the door, the opening of the field. "It is so near the heart,/an eternal pasture folded in all thought," writes Robert

Duncan in the poem "Often I Am Permitted to Return to a Meadow," from which I took this book's epigraph. Not automatically, but out of the search for recognition, for mutuality. A mutuality that is most often asymmetrical: the analyst recognizes the patient's truth, the patient recognizes the analyst's skill and intention.

As a poet and a psychoanalytically informed psychotherapist, I came rather late in my life to the realization that my two endeavors shared a common proposition. I think, retrospectively, I was guarding my avocation from the intrusion of my vocation. It took my becoming secure that my poet self would not desert me in the face of life's stresses before I was willing to let it share a room with my therapist self.

It is to my long apprenticeship and friendship with the English-born American poet Denise Levertov (1923–1997) that I owe my dedication to the refinement of perception, to the pursuit of the actual. "The authentic!" she writes,

> It rolls
> just out of reach, beyond
> running feet and
> stretching fingers, down
> the green slope and into
> the black waves of the sea.
> (2013, p. 172, "Matins")

The actual inheres, she maintains, quoting Hopkins; it carves out a space in the mind, an *inscape*. "Oh blessed be," Denise exclaims, on a walk near my house in the Berkeley Hills, seeing a perfect iris poking through a splintered wood fence. A ballet girl again, she breaks off a plié.

The door into the second space can be beauty, but it can also be a naming of brutality, as when William Blake nails the hypocrisy of the self-satisfied vicars, "wise guardians of the poor" (1970, p. 13), who bless the children on Holy Thursday but ignore them the rest of the time. The poem names their wrong but feels right. It offers aesthetic pleasure to accompany our moral outrage. It is this quality of rightness that works its way in us, opening a space of self-reflection, deflating a bit our unearned self-regard.

My psychoanalytic heroes, Heinz Kohut, Robert Stolorow and Beatrice Beebe, share with the poets a search for the actual, a distrust of reification. Kohut, whom I knew only through writings and contacts with his colleagues, bent the arc of psychoanalysis back toward humanism, toward empathic connection, toward an immersion in the moment-to-moment vicissitudes of his patients' lived experience. An attitude of humility, not arrogance, underlying his approach: "I realized," he wrote, musing on times when he disagreed with his patients, "that my rightness was superficial, while theirs was profound" (1984, p. 94). Stolorow, along with his colleague George Atwood and others, helped finish Kohut's transformation of psychoanalysis from a theory of the Cartesian, isolated mind to an exploration of the intersubjective field that emerges in the analytic encounter. And Beebe, in her infant research, elaborated the pragmatics of intersubjectivity and elucidated the dyadic origin of self and relationship.

I believe that each of these three, though not poets themselves – along with their many colleagues in the relational psychoanalytic world – helped create a more poetic psychoanalysis. Not in the usual sense of drawing, as Freud did, from poetry and myth to conceptualize the nature of human existence. More through the application of the poet's sensibility, the poet's inventiveness and the odd mix of humility and boldness that underlies the poet's endeavor. This is the project I hereby turn to. It has been integrative for me; I hope that readers of many backgrounds will find the exploration of poetry I offer useful in their lives and in their healing practices.

Part I

Chapter 1

The poetics of psychoanalytic treatment

Several years ago at a psychoanalytic conference, I heard George Atwood (1997), who works with a very disturbed client population, discuss the difficulty of accepting a psychotic patient's statement, "I am dead." It is so easy to miss the patient's attempts to communicate poetically what is otherwise incommunicable. If we listen poetically, it is not, or not only, the conviction of nonexistence that the statement communicates. Our imagination supplies a shared sense of what this statement omits, a pulsing, thwarted desire to be alive, truncated by the monosyllabic rhythm of the statement, a three-note descent to the portals of hell: "I am dead."

As a psychotherapist who is also a poet, I often think of the similarities between my two endeavors. Psychoanalysis has long been a source for literary interpretation. In this chapter, I propose to reverse the direction of inquiry and look at analytic treatment through the lens of four topics in poetics: metaphor, image, sound and rhythm and form. I will conclude with a discussion of the way an ear for poetry informed my treatment of Lisa, a 36-year-old patient who had an extremely traumatic childhood.

The therapist's two primary activities, listening to patients and making interpretations, are both abetted by a poet's sensibility. There is a strong resemblance between the kind of alert reverie one falls into under the spell of a poem – combining both a heightened sense of meaning and the lulling trance of sound and rhythm – and the way one listens to both the content and the nonverbal aspects of patients' communication. Effective interpretations draw on the same language skills – concision, clarity, allusiveness – that inform the best poems.

But the analogy goes farther than that. The intersubjective field a poem creates between writer and reader, a field of language charged with meaning, bears a strong resemblance to the language-mediated intersubjective field (Atwood and Stolorow, 1984) created by the analyst and patient. A successful poem, like a successful interpretation (Stolorow, 1993), creates a sense of intersubjective relatedness. Nobel Laureate Seamus Heaney quotes Jorge Luis Borges to advance this view of poetry: "Poetry lies in the meeting of poem and reader, not in the lines and symbols printed on pages of a book. What is essential is . . . the thrill, the almost physical emotion that comes with each reading" (1995, p. 8).

Poets often make the argument that poetry can provide a cure for despair and isolation. William Carlos Williams writes, "It is difficult/to get the news from poems/yet men die miserably every day/for lack/of what is found there" (1962, pp. 161–162). Adrienne Rich writes that "Poetry can break open locked chambers of possibility, restore numbed zones of feeling, recharge desire" (1993, p. xiv). In providing a bridge between subjective worlds, poetry is inherently a blow against what Stolorow and Atwood (1992) call "the myth of the isolated mind." How can therapists tap into this curative power?

The poetry therapy movement has argued for the inclusion of poetry in the therapy process. Theodore Reik has argued for "a poetic approach to depth psychology. The psychologist should be like an actor who learns technique only to forget it once he is on stage" (1968, p. 6). What I propose here is not to make therapy more "poetic" but to extend our understanding of the therapy process by looking at it through the lens of poetics.

Metaphor

I begin with metaphor because it is so central to the creation of a sense of intersubjective relatedness. The word metaphor's origin in the Greek *metapherein*, to transfer, reveals its essential task: to transfer objects from the external world into the world of the poem. Metaphors exist in the transitional space (Winnicott, 1971a) between object and subject. As the critic Northrup Frye points out:

> literature always assumes, in its metaphors, a relation between human consciousness and its natural environment that passes beyond – in fact, outrages and violates – the ordinary common sense based on a permanent separation of subject and object.
>
> (1990a, p. 71)

This violation of the boundaries between object and subject is analogous to Kohut's (1966) description of the artist's sense of complete oneness with objects in his environment: "Like the air which we breathe, they are most clearly experienced at the moment of union with the self" (p. 255).

When Homer (1990), in Book 8 of the *Iliad*, compares the watchfires of the Greek and Trojan armies to "Stars in the night sky glittering/round the moon's brilliant blaze in all their glory/when the air falls to a sudden, windless calm" (p. 249), he is linking his empathic understanding of the soldiers' experience of a calm night before battle to the reader's experience of the awe and terror a still, clear night can inspire. Stars and watchfires, objects in the natural world, have been transferred into the intersubjective field of the poem. We do not read poetry primarily as evidence of the poet's strange or enlightened consciousness; we read poetry to leave our own isolation and enter a communal world based on shared meanings.

Our patients' metaphoric communications are often unelaborated or merely alluded to. When Atwood's patient says to him "I am dead," there is an implied comparison of a completely alienated self-state and a corpse. Ironically, this metaphor of a corpse in the room, with its coldness and stench, is a living conduit through which a moment of intersubjective relatedness flows.

A metaphoric interpretation can similarly create intersubjective conjunction. In interpreting a patient's description of continually returning with new hope to her intrusive and narcissistic mother, only to be disappointed again, I said, "It's like a piece of candy with a delicious chocolate coating, but a center you don't like; you think you can just eat the chocolate, but somehow the filling, no matter how little you actually bite into it, ends up dominating the taste." The candy metaphor comes to stand for my understanding of her relationship with her mother: the arousal in the anticipation of getting her needs met, the hope that she can somehow master the relationship and just "bite deep enough" and the way disappointment comes to dominate the experience like an underlying flavor that lasts in the mouth. But the metaphor is more than just a shorthand referent to a complex pathological tie. If I have made a successful interpretation, it is my own knowledge of hunger and disappointment that I have communicated.

Metaphors are an example of what contemporary psychoanalysts (e.g., Ogden, 1995) describe as an emergent third. It emerges between object and subject or between two subjects. The watchfires/night sky metaphor becomes a third, a common fate both Greeks and Trojans are under. The candy metaphor I offer my patient reorganizes our work. We are now the people who understand her relationship to her mother in this particular way.

A retreat from poetry: concretization and reification

Both therapists and patients are likely to retreat from the shared conjunction of metaphorical space into the relative safety of the literal and concrete. In this, they are enacting, or reenacting, a retreat from a self sustained by selfobject relationships into a self sustained by concretization and reification. Such a retreat accomplishes two goals. It shores up a shakily organized subjective world and it withdraws from a potentially disappointing relationship into the protection of a separate and inviolable belief in the objective reality of one's thoughts and feelings (Stolorow, Brandchaft, and Atwood, 1987). Concretization is a universal hallmark of subjective experience, but it comes to dominate psychic organization when "early, validating responsiveness has been consistently absent or grossly unreliable" (p. 133). Then a retreat to the literal, or to the compulsive, as in psychosexual enactments, dominates and isolates psychic life. One way of understanding the therapy process is to see it as elevating concretizations into metaphors, vehicles of shared understanding. Adequate therapeutic treatment lifts the patient's communications out of their literal heaviness and lets them "float" in the room as mutually held conduits for understanding. In this sense a life of rigidly held, even delusional, beliefs, a life of compulsive sexual enactments or psychosomatizations, is a life without poetry. And from my perspective as poet and therapist, I would add it is a life in search of poetry – of a metaphor replete with shared meanings.

If patients are prone to reduce metaphors to the literal, therapists are prone to move in the opposite direction, to elevate metaphors into reified universal truths. Reification involves a withdrawal from the poetic, from the intersubjective. To speak of a patient's Oedipus complex as something that exists as an entity is to withdraw from the intersubjective power of metaphor, as when a patient's description of being "shot down" when he asked his father for a loan interacts with the therapist's own construction of meanings (based perhaps on trace memories of his own childhood shame and rage, his reading in a college survey course of Sophocles's shocking play, his reading of Freud and subsequent theorists). The reification of metaphors withdraws them from the intersubjective field and coats them with a kind of pseudoscientific Teflon. Metaphors, on the other hand, are adhesive: they draw meanings to them.

Image

Image differs from metaphor by virtue of the lack of intent behind it. Whereas a metaphor carries the intent of the maker to communicate his or her subjectivity, an image stands alone. It is the act of perception itself that infuses an image with subjective meaning. "Images haunt," writes the poet Robert Hass. "Images are not quite ideas; they are stiller than that, with less implication outside themselves. And they are not myth, they do not have that explanatory power; they are closer to pure story" (1984, p. 275).

Hass's notion that images are closer to pure story is very relevant to our understanding of a patient's retrieval of powerful images from dreams, from memory or from intensely felt daily perceptions. In the first dream reported by a young male patient suffering from obsessive thoughts about his own well-being as well as elaborate compulsive rituals, he described "Huge boulders. They're not moving but there's a sense of danger, like we could be crushed at any moment. My father is with me." It was enormously tempting to interpret these boulders, to convert them to metaphors. But to do so would be to lose the narrative force that they could communicate: "I am in terrible danger from something overwhelmingly heavy. My father is with me, but he's in danger too." Of course, I am integrating these boulders into my own subjective schema, imagining them to be symbols of the way masculinity was crushed in my patient's household by the cold, critical mother he has just begun talking about. Such organizing activity, however necessary to the therapy process, is a step away from a moment of intersubjective relatedness of shared perception the image affords: *boulders*.

Sound and rhythm

The last twenty years or so have seen a marked increase in interest in nonverbal forms of communication in psychotherapy (Stern et al., 1998). This thinking focuses on the patient's nonverbal communication of affect-states and on the way the therapist's nonverbal responses influence the patient's sense of attachment. Confirmation that intersubjective relatedness is woven from sounds and rhythm comes from infant research (Stern, 1985; Beebe and Lachmann, 1992, 2002). These researchers found caregivers conveying affect-attunement by mirroring the rhythm and tone of the infant's expressions. Similarly, affect regulation was achieved by "changing the music" and replaying it with a different rhythm or intensity. Knoblauch (2000) sees a strong analogy between the therapy process and the improvisational dialog of jazz. What light can an understanding of the "music" of poetry shed on this inquiry?

Ezra Pound defined three sources of poetry's power. Along with the play of meanings in the words themselves (which Pound called *logopoeia*) and the play of images we have just discussed (which Pound called *phanopoeia*), he described "*melopoeia*: wherein the words are charged, over and above their plain meaning, with some musical property, which directs the bearing or trend of that meaning" (1968, p. 25).

It would seem at first glance that this melopoeia would have the least applicability to psychotherapy of the poetic concepts; after all, it is the poet's intention to charge his language with melody and rhythm, while everyday discourse, including therapeutic discourse, is free of this intention. However, when we understand that sound and rhythm are among the primary ways poetry connects subjective worlds, their relevance is more apparent. Pound describes melopoeia as having "a contrary current, a force tending to lull or distract the reader from the exact sense of the language. It is poetry on the borders of music and music is perhaps the bridge between consciousness and the unthinking sentient or even insentient universe" (p. 26). When William Blake writes "Ah Sun-flower, weary of time,/Who countest the steps of the sun," a prime source of the poem's meaning comes from the way the elongated vowels of pure longing in the first line bump into the truncated rhythms of time-bound reality in the second.

If it is through sound and rhythm that our patients communicate their affect states, then an ear attuned to the poetry of speech will be better able to receive these communications. Poets know that long syllables communicate yearning or sadness; short syllables communicate haste or excitement. Hard consonants convey boundaries or limitations. The alternation in a poem between rapid phrasing and slower cadences often mirrors a dialectical clash of meanings, such as a yearning for transcendence and the inevitable fact of mortality in Blake's "Sunflower" poem.

Meerloo (1968) speaks of the rhythm of speech as a kind of "mental contagion." Most therapists are aware of the way a downwardly inflected sentence that trails off into silence reveals an abyss; the therapist's silence or slowly worded reply conveys through sound and rhythm an intersubjective sharing of this abyss.

Form

The terms "intersubjectivity," and, by extension the "intersubjective field," refer not to a specific kind of relationship but to the inevitable product of the interaction of two differing subjectivities (Orange, Atwood, and Stolorow, 1997). This field has no *a priori* form or boundary. The discovery of form in an analysis gives shape and boundary to the field, and, I would argue, is one source of meaning and healing in the analytic process. Stephen Mitchell states that in psychoanalysis, "[T]he organizational scheme arrived at is a dual creation, shaped partly by the patient's material but also shaped inevitably by the analyst's patterns of thought or theory" (1993, p. 58). He goes on to quote the literary critic Frank Kermode as saying "[the analyst] might more usefully be thought of as a kind of a poet rather than as a kind of archaeologist." Form in poetry grows out of the poet's encounter with his subject matter; in therapy, form emerges from the encounter between patient and therapist.

Form in poetry is a source of aesthetic pleasure. We admire a poem's shape, its spareness or opulence. We are comforted by the repetitions in patterns of rhythm or structure, we are surprised by variations. But form also conveys a deeper meaning, a discovery of something both inevitable and transcendent. Denise Levertov writes of "an intuition of an order, a form beyond forms, in which forms partake, and of which man's creative works are analogies, natural allegories" (1992, p. 68). I believe it is the discovery of this form that Robert Duncan is referring to when he writes, in the poem I used as an epigraph to the book, that it is "a given property of the mind/that certain properties hold against chaos" (1960, p. 7). It is precisely here that we can apply the concept of form to psychoanalysis. The intersubjective meaning of form in an analysis is that something bounded, shapely and deeply meaningful can be created out of the therapist's encounter with the patient.

Poetic theory divides form into two categories: received or traditional forms and organic forms, in which the form is discovered as inherent in the content. I would argue that there are analogies to both in the psychoanalytic process. The repetitive patterns of scheduling, of seating, of payment, of opening and closing sessions provide order and recognition (i.e., this is the form of analysis, this is what it's like). These received or ritualistic forms connect the intersubjective field with a sense of history: "this is the way other analyses have taken place, ours will take its place in that history."

The improvised or discovered forms in therapy are equally important: idiosyncratic rituals for beginning or ending sessions, the way affect builds and is dissipated in sessions, the distribution of attention between reports of recent experience, remembrances of childhood and transference topics. These provide a shape to each individual analysis.

A good part of the significance of these elements of "improvised" form derives from the fact that they are created collaboratively. In commenting on *A Nest of Ninnies*, an experimental collaborative novel by James Schuyler and John Ashberry, David Lehman writes, "The extraordinary thing . . . is that the two poets have dissolved their two personalities and merged so entirely into a common style that the book's author is neither Schuyler nor Ashberry but a third entity fashioned in the process of collaboration" (1998, p. 82). This "third entity" is analogous to Ogden's (1995) notion of the "analytic third," as well as to Kohut's (1985) concept of the "group self" or to the "mutual self" of couples (Shaddock, 2000). There is profound meaning for therapist and patient alike in the way this group self guides and shapes the course of therapy.

Case example

Lisa is an attractive, successful, 36-year-old senior executive in a national retail company. For a time, I, as a therapist, was in a kind of thrall to her beauty. But later, as the full dimension of her struggles became clearer, it seemed a kind of irony. She has been in treatment for six years, minus a one-year break after the second year. Lisa's style belies a life of desperation in which she is beset by convictions of her utter badness. She would defend against them with shopping binges that would put her severely into debt. But these binges only heightened her conviction of her badness, which then manifested in near-psychotic suicidal ideation characterized by a voice saying, "die Lisa die." This ideation has led to several suicide attempts, the most serious of which came during the time when she had stopped treatment. In that incident, her then-husband found her nearly unconscious in the bathroom with a plastic bag over her head; he ripped it off and proceeded to yell at her and berate her for "being so stupid." Lisa defended against the belief in her innate badness with dissociation, relentless perfectionism and a grandiose belief in her psychic powers.

Lisa grew up on a ranch, the middle of three sisters. Her mother was manic-depressive, with long periods of depression punctuated by brief manic episodes. She was also alcoholic, which deepened her symptomology on both ends of her mood swings. Lisa experienced further trauma from her verbally and physically abusive maternal grandmother and her paternal grandfather, who lived in an outbuilding on the ranch and molested all the daughters. Lisa's intelligence and good looks led the family to turn to her for salvation: she was a mother to her mother and her younger sister and a favorite of her father, who relied on her for companionship around the ranch until he died of a sudden heart attack when she was 11. Thereafter, family life became completely chaotic: Lisa grew up "on the streets" of a nearby town; her mother would disappear for days at a time. Tellingly, Lisa always tried to hide her shameful existence behind her academic achievements and good looks.

The treatment can be summarized as having three phases. The initial phase was characterized by my active, and – given the ever-present threat of suicide – rather desperate attempts to make interpretations that would help her, while the gap between her outer life of achievement and her inner torment and shame grew ever wider. There were times during this phase when Lisa was very dissociated – she would end sessions in a far-off voice that said, "Well, I've got to go now."

Following an abrupt and premature termination (which she later characterized as needing to get away from me so I wouldn't feel responsible when she killed herself), Lisa returned to treatment. She had recently separated from her husband. During this second phase, Lisa began to describe the "living hell" of her emotionally abusive and sexually exploitive relationship with her husband. She also discussed childhood memories of sexual abuse and shame about her mother. This period was characterized by much lower interpretive activity on my part.

During the fifth year of treatment, Lisa moved to a large East Coast city. Our work has continued on the phone. The phone sessions, which have now gone on for more than a year, constitute a third phase of the treatment. This phase has been characterized by collaboration: a mutual understanding of her childhood trauma and a gradual testing, with many false starts, of the possibility that she might not be completely unlovable after all. As of this writing, she is engaged to a man who, though loving, is also moody and given to bouts of unexplained withdrawal and anger.

With this summary, I will now proceed to discuss aspects of the case from the point of view of my discussion of metaphor, image, sound and rhythm and form.

Metaphor: skin hunger

Shortly after moving to the East Coast, Lisa came up with a metaphor to describe the need that kept leading her to affairs with inappropriate men. "I call it *skin hunger*. Sometimes I need to be touched and held so bad I can't bear it. I don't care about sex. I just can't stand the skin hunger."

Lisa and I had speculated together that there was a layer of psychic pain deeper than the shame about the molestation and her mother's alcoholism. We had discussed it in terms of her relationship to her gravely emotionally disabled younger sister, who in her 30s was still living at home with her mother. She saw how her sister's problems originated in her mother's depressed absences. Lisa's coming up with this metaphor signaled that she was ready to look at her own terrible experiences of abandonment.

But her production of this metaphor did more than that – it radically altered the intersubjective field between therapist and patient by simultaneously dissolving her defensive grandiosity and my paternal countertransference. I felt a shift inside myself almost immediately after she came up with the metaphor. I felt less edgy, less responsible, sadder. I realized retrospectively that her great beauty and largely unvoiced desperation had always provoked a confused response in me – conflated of my own defensive grandiosity ("I've got what it takes to help her") and a desperate wish to take away her pain. The shift I now experienced was facilitated by the way the metaphor reached under her own eroticized transferences to express the infantile neediness they hid.

This was accomplished both by the evocative power of her metaphor itself and by the developmental achievement it announced. To understand the evocative power of this metaphor, we need only to think of what would have been lost if Lisa had said, "I just feel an overwhelming desire for skin contact" instead. By contrast, this metaphor created in me an image of all the pores in skin as infant's mouths, a surface of need that completely surrounded her.

The safety that allowed for my surrender to this moment of intersubjective conjunction came in part from the developmental achievement it represented for Lisa. After five years of treatment, she was able to invent a metaphor for her utter deprivation, to bring it into the field of treatment rather than concretize it in shopping binges and suicide attempts. We have referred to "skin hunger" many times since. Each time, it evokes both an image of endless hunger and our pleasure at having named and, at least partially, mastered it.

Image: the look

Shortly after she brought in the metaphor of skin hunger, Lisa produced a childhood memory that was more specific and vivid than others:

> I was thinking the other morning of something that used to happen. I must have been three or four. My mother used to disappear for hours. I'd go look for her because my sister would be crying and I'd find her in the basement, watching TV. When I'd find her, she'd look at me with this look of surprise and hurt like a child who's been caught being bad. I can still see that look. It just turns my stomach to think about it.

This image of her mother's look functioned very much like Robert Hass's notion of "pure story." It told of the terrible bind Lisa had been in as a child, torn between rage at her mother's self-indulgence and betrayal on the one hand and the guilt Lisa felt for not providing the parental reassurance her child-mother so desperately needed. And it told of something perhaps even more troubling: the terrible shame at the very core of her mother's existence. I too had a visceral response to the look, and I was about to comment on my understanding when Lisa continued, "You know, I believed for the longest time that the only way to get away from that look was to die. I guess I don't feel that so much anymore." At this point, I felt that any interpretation on my part would diminish the act of perception we were sharing.

The image of her mother's look became a reliable source of intersubjective relatedness in therapy. From the first time Lisa mentioned the look, our mutual understanding of its meaning felt solid rather than exploratory. We would refer to it when Lisa was in the throes of a repetition of her childhood dilemma, either with her emotionally disabled sister or with one of the men she was dating. Our shared understanding of the trauma the image evoked provided for Lisa a development-enhancing secondary ameliorative response (Stolorow and Atwood, 1992). In contrast to her often dissociated self states, the image grounded Lisa's subjective experience with a starkly clear sense of reality.

One detail of Lisa's remembrance merited particular exploration. Lisa had only gone and looked for her mother in the basement because her sister was crying. At three or four, she was already a little mother. We came to see that this mother role helped consolidate a shaky sense of self. This memory was of a time when her mother's look overwhelmed her little-mother-self, and she felt the full devastation of her mother's absence. The metaphor of skin hunger and the image of her mother's look thus came to provide a kind of map to Lisa's childhood experience.

Sound and rhythm

In about the middle of the fourth year of treatment, Lisa reported the following dream: "I'm in a house, and you're chasing after me. Not running, but deliberately. Room after room. Finally I go hide in a closet. You come after me. I'm not afraid you'll hurt me, only that . . . under my clothes . . . you'll find I . . . don't . . . exist at all." I've deliberately chosen an example that has such manifest and profound transference meanings because I want to demonstrate the way that the sound and rhythm of Lisa's speech functioned, in Pound's terms, as a "contrary current" to some of the content. Taken up by the pursuit content and responding to the more frantic rhythm of the earlier part of the dream, I responded, unemphatically, "It's about therapy, isn't it? It's about my trying to understand you, and your fear of being exposed. Perhaps the dream has come to show us where we need to go." At this point Lisa made, through the deliberate slowness of her statement and the quietness of her voice, another attempt to regulate my affect: "What if . . . I . . . don't want to . . . ?" Her repetition of this slow cadence and downward inflection had the desired effect: I was pierced by the emotional content of her words: "under my clothes . . . I don't . . . exist . . . at all." Unconsciously matching her speech rhythm, I replied, "Then we'll stay . . . here . . . as long . . . as we need to."

It was Lisa's speech rhythm's that revealed the heart of the dream: despite the allusions to pursuit, hiding, sex and even rape, the dream was about revealing to me the utter desolation at the core of her existence. The contrast between slow and fast speech rhythms in this dialog mirrored the contrast between the beginning and later stages of therapy: the former characterized by acting out and a desperate attempt for therapeutic effectiveness, the latter by the slow and somber unfolding of the story of her traumatic childhood.

Form

The later stage of therapy was characterized by much less interpretive activity on my part. Often I would make a single genetic interpretation in a session, as if to ground our discussion of the present in the context of her traumatic past. Lisa would pause a moment and then continue her story. This is an example of a mutually derived formal convention.

Retrospectively, it seems that the entire therapy had been guided by some formal principles. Recently, Lisa said, "It's so easy to talk now. You say something and I say something. I remember when I could barely talk at all. I'd come to a place before the end of the session, and it would be, 'Time to go now.' And then, it seemed all I could do was cry. I wondered if it was so easy to talk now because we were on the phone, and you couldn't see how I looked. But when I saw you in your office, it was the same, and I knew that things had really changed." I replied, "It is comforting that things have evolved. It seems that, for all of our struggles, we were on the right track."

Lisa and I were trying to express, with this interaction, our appreciation that the treatment had been guided by some intrinsic form. A symphonic metaphor occurs to me. The phases of the treatment are like movements, beginning with a scherzo of my active and increasingly desperate attempts to help Lisa and her equally frantic attempts to shore herself up in the face of growing desperation. The yearlong break in treatment must be included here as one of the "movements": a terrible, almost unendurable silence. And then the adagio of her retrieval of childhood memories of abuse and neglect, as well as her processing the breakup of her marriage – and my own, uncharacteristic quiet. And finally the emergence of a dialog, a sharing of themes. That Lisa's subjective world of chaos and annihilating self-hatred could enter the intersubjective field of treatment and experience a sense of order and aesthetic rightness was enormously important to both of us. Lisa had a highly developed aesthetic sense, but her relentless quest for personal beauty was largely defensive and often self-destructive. The growing awareness that our work together has had its own form conveyed to Lisa that beauty and meaning did not require a sequestering of past trauma but in fact could grow out of her terrible childhood experiences.

In conclusion, I would stress that I am in no way arguing for poetry as a substitute for rigorous analytic exploration. I hope I have demonstrated here, though, that an attention to the poetic aspects of analytic discourse, especially metaphor, image, sound and rhythm and form, offers unique opportunities for discovering, facilitating and communicating moments of intersubjective conjunction.

With these four topics – metaphor, image, sound and rhythm and form – in mind, let us now turn to the question of whether poetry and the poetic process can lend themselves to specific topics in treatment, such as the role of creativity in the analytic process, which we turn to in the next chapter.

Chapter 2

To build a new world

Creative and aesthetic choices in psychoanalysis

> . . . A new world
> Is only a new mind.
> And the mind and the poem
> Are all apiece.
> (William Carlos Williams, 1991b)

What to say? Should I just stay silent? How much should what I say reflect what I just heard? How much of my own thoughts or interpretations should I include? Though we don't think of an analytic session as a composition, compositional decisions are made in every moment. Theoretical or practical constraints govern those decisions. Including a decision to, as much as possible, not be governed by preexisting constraints. Artist/analyst Julia Schwartz writes:

> One thing in common about painting and psychoanalysis: it doesn't matter where you begin, it only matters where you go. Or maybe that you begin at all. It's about the process, about making the painting, including all the mistakes and false starts and dead ends.
>
> (2017, p. 140)

A mother cooing and reacting to her baby. A dancer responding to the floor as if it were a living being. A single word on the space of the page dictating all the aesthetic decisions that come after it. Artists organize their composition through a series of moment-to-moment aesthetic decisions. And they, in turn, are organized by those decisions.

Contemporary psychoanalytic theory views the therapy process as co-created by the patient and analyst. In searching for ways to describe the analyst's contribution to this process, contemporary thinkers have used analogies to improvisational theater (Ringstrom, 2001), to free jazz (Knoblauch, 2000), to poetry (Shaddock, 2010) and to the regulatory interaction of caregivers and infants (Beebe and Lachmann, 2002). These analogies emphasize the dyadic nature of the treatment process and highlight the spontaneous, improvisational nature of the analyst's responses.

This chapter examines the role of creativity in the analytic process by comparing the moment-to-moment decisions that go into the process of composing a poem with the moment-to-moment decisions in an analytic session. In order to elucidate the analogy between the creative process in poetry and psychoanalysis, I will describe the making of a single one of my poems, "Asymptote" (Shaddock, 2012), and then I will describe how I made a clinical decision in the treatment of a 57-year-old man who was struggling with issues around his father.

The content and process of a therapy session emerge from the dyadic therapist/patient system. But this system is not delineated by the walls of the consulting room. Everything that has happened in both the patient and the therapists' life is part of the context, as well as everything in human history, and everything that is currently happening in the world around them. The precursors to a coordination of looks and nods, a few words of interpretation or encouragement, are unimaginably complex.

In order to see the analogy between the dyadic therapy process and the composition of a poem, we must reconceptualize the idea of the isolated artist and see the composition process as likewise emerging from a series of dyadic relationships. The first of these dyads is internal: the composition process is a dialogue between the poet and his own unconscious mind. The poet first "listens" to the products his imagination presents and then moves in to make conscious aesthetic decisions that shape the poem toward a desired form. In the language of dynamic systems theory (Thelan and Smith, 1994), the poem is an emergent property of the dynamic interaction of the two subsystems of imaginative flow and conscious intent.

The second of these dyads shows the poem as emerging between the poet and the world around him. In her essay "The Poet in the World," Denise Levertov writes:

[the poet] has sat in the bathtub listening to Bach's *St. Mathew's Passion*, he has looked up from the death of Socrates, disturbed by some extra noise amid the jarring and lurching of the subway train and the many rhythmic rattling of its parts, and seen one man stab another and a third spring from his seat and assist the wounded one.

Breaking into verse herself, Levertov continues: "Slowly men and women move in life,/cumbered./The passing of sorrow, the passing/of joy. All awareness//is the awareness of time" (1992, pp. 132–133). As we shall see when I describe the composition of the poem "Asymptote," the poet interrogates the world around him, demanding that it yield up its meanings. But the poet also allows the world to enter him, through odd moments of perception, ironies and coincidences.

The third dialog from which the poem emerges is a dialog with literary tradition. No matter how new or inventive seeming, each poem emerges as a response to predecessors, and each poem ripples the pond of literary history, sending its waves forward to alter its successors and also backward, altering our understanding of the past. As we noted in our discussion of form in psychoanalysis in the last chapter, even the relatively new practice of psychoanalysis takes its form from the history of analyses that have preceded it.

Though Hagman (2005, 2015) has argued that aesthetic choices do play an important role in the analytic process, the analyst's responses are not primarily driven by aesthetic considerations. We forego some sense of eloquence in favor of language that "fits" the moment. The analyst's *attitude* (Coburn, 2014) – derived from theory, philosophy and personal experience – does play an analogous role in shaping his responses to the patient. Open minded, open to the energy of the moment, open to his own fallibility, the contemporary analyst's attitude organizes the moment-to-moment flow and overall trajectory of the work.

Most of the time, both the artist's compositional constraints and the analyst's therapeutic attitude operate in the background. "Real-time" compositional or therapeutic decisions may be so rapid as to blur the distinction between listening and responding. My method here will be to employ the luxury of retrospective inquiry to the composition of a single poem and to a clinical decision in a brief case vignette.

I would make the disclaimer before proceeding that I am not trying to create a hard and fast analogy between the two different endeavors that I find myself engaged in on an almost daily basis. Rather, I am exploring the overlap between the two activities in the hope that an examination of my process as a poet can shed light into some unexamined corners of the analytic process. To this end, I place them side by side.

The making of the poem "Asymptote"

The Romantic notion – as exemplified by William Blake's assertion that his poems were dictated to him by his deceased brother – holds that the creative process involves an act of reception or surrender to a larger force. By Contrast, I see the creative process is an alternation between surrender (to the unconscious, to chance) and focused effort and attention. My process of composing "Asymptote" illustrates this alternation. I chose "Asymptote" to discuss because it has a philosophical affinity with my approach to analytic treatment. The title evokes a hermeneutic, constructivist approach to human understanding, and the poem itself moves by fits and starts toward its own conclusion rather than offering some great resolution or epiphany. My approach to a patient's inner world is asymptotic: I may get closer, but I will never actually touch it.

I hope to show here that the poet's attention to the alternation of will and surrender, his attention to energy, sound and rhythm and his attention to that mysterious sense of wholeness we call form might be useful components of the therapist's tool chest.

Here is the poem in full:

> Asymptote
> Little chickens jump on spoons
> to play a wineglass xylophone.
> I'd been reading a book on hermeneutics
> when Cartoon Network mysteriously clicked on.
> Puffy mice join in the raucous chorus.
> Is language, Gadamer asks, a bridge or a barrier?
> A bridge he maintains, through which
> we can know ourselves in the being of the other.
> When her husband left her my neighbor
> spent days sorting bolts and screws:
> number four hex heads, half round number sixes.
> It seems to me we're approaching God
> as an asymptote. Our calculations are getting
> ever more precise, but we are running out of time.

Eventually she moved to Oregon, just kept driving
until she found a place she liked, in, no kidding,
Sweet Home. *The fusion of horizons* is Gadamer's telling
phrase for the nature of understanding.
The kitchen fills up with chicks
and mice for the madcap crescendo:
they pop out of drawers, poke
through the flute of the teakettle (2012, p. 559).

The origin of the poem was a line in a notebook that came to me a long
time before I actually used it: "We are approaching God as an asymptote."
I don't know where the line came from; its source lies in the workings
of what poets call the imagination and psychoanalysis has traditionally
called the creative unconscious (Sachs, 1942). It is a mental product of
the sort that Hans Sachs following Freud (1908) tellingly called "the community of daydreams." Whatever the source, I had the feeling that I was
onto something as I copied that line into a notebook. In the next phase of
preparation, I began to consciously pursue the meanings and references
the line suggested. Surrender alternating with will. This phase took me
several months. My exploration of the phrase, which emerged from the
unconscious or stream of consciousness, bears some analogy to the psychoanalytic exploration of a quip, slip or dream image.

An asymptote is a line that the graph of an equation approaches but does
not intersect. For example, in the graph of $y = 1/x$, the line approaches the
x-axis ($y = 0$), but never touches it. As the value of x increases, the frac-
tion the function describes will grow ever smaller, but the curve will never
reach $y = 0$. If you Google asymptote, as I did, you will find examples from
math and physics, but also from design and architecture.

The idea of an asymptote serves as a metaphor for the relationship of
faith (or at least my faith) to God: we can get closer and closer, but we will
never get all the way there. To some, this may seem disappointing, but for
me, it is quite a consoling notion, as if the spiritual journey were an end in
itself. In the Jewish mystical tradition of Kabbalah, *ain soph*, the highest
level that human consciousness may attain, remains ineffable.

In addition to the theological considerations the line posed, there was
a philosophical dimension. I realized that the line reflected a hermeneutic approach to faith and understanding in which meaning is never absolute but emerges from engagement, through dialog and interpretation

(Stolorow, Atwood, and Orange, 2002; Orange, 2010). A hermeneutic sensibility plays a big part in my approach to therapy as well. It was while I was doing a little reading up on hermeneutic philosophy that the incident that became the point of departure for the poem took place, with hilarity and surprise.

I don't know if it was a hidden timer in the set or a signal from a random remote, but I was deeply trying to decode a hermeneutic text when the set in the other room turned itself on to one of those old-time "Silly Symphony" pieces that Cartoon Network uses to fill the daytime hours while the kids are presumably in school. My son must have been furtively watching that channel after bedtime the night before.

The chance juxtaposition of these two different human endeavors, philosophy and cartooning, struck me as an example of hermeneutics at play, in which meaning is derived from the layering of different interpretations and subjectivities. Gadamer, who wrote "The essence of the question is the opening up, and keeping open of possibilities," might have been delighted at the chickens' kitchen symphony.

After some experimenting around, I realized that I would let the juxtaposition of these two events set the form of the poem – it would be a poem of juxtapositions rather than explicit connections. A bit more postmodern than I usually allow myself to go. So then I associated (in retrospect, I must have been musing on the possibility, or impossibility, of language to create understanding) to a memory I had of dropping in on my neighbor soon after her husband announced that he had fallen in love with another woman and was leaving her. I decided to include that memory in the poem, with its chilling image of her desperately trying to sort out her world by sorting a random collection of nuts and bolts into jars. I added the happier ending to her story later, after I heard about it from a mutual friend.

So far I had been proceeding intuitively, but next came a formal decision. In the poems about faith (or the lack of it) that I was writing at that time, I quite often buried a direct statement of faith in the middle of a poem, surrounded by observations or other associations. This formal device appealed to me because it mimicked my own faith – it was just one component of my thought stream – recurring (and sometimes reassuring me) from time to time. I think the mix of indirection and direct statement the poem evinces bears a resemblance to my therapy interpretations. Hoping as always, for a little magic: a bit of Gadamer, a bit of "Silly Symphony," a roll of "K" sounds: kitchen, chicks, madcap, crescendo, to take me out.

This poem is a gesture of hope for order in the face of disorder and anxiety, a gesture that indicates that, out of the randomness of events and the randomness of our intentions – poking our heads, as it were, out of the teakettle and singing like mad – some meaning emerges. Not certainty or an overpowering belief in God, but at least a sense of process, that we are getting somewhere in our ongoing attempt to, in Wallace Stevens's (1978, p. 76) words "order the slovenly universe."

I have sought through this description of writing "Asymptote" to elucidate the dialectic in the creative process between intention and discovery. Guiding both sides of this dialectic is the poet's own aesthetic judgment. The poet seeks to facilitate the emergence of a language act that is coherent and aesthetically pleasing and carries meaning. To examine the analogy between this creative act and the process of conducting a psychoanalytically informed treatment, I would like to present the following case vignette.

The case of Dan

Psychoanalytic case reports are, like accounts of poetic composition, perforce reconstructions. What I will attempt to get at with the case of Dan are elements of my therapeutic process and decision making, ones that are at best half conscious.

Dan is a 57-year-old man, slight of build but very fit and well dressed, who works as an executive for a governmental agency. His presenting problem was dissatisfaction with his work situation, specifically with his boss, who he described as highly narcissistic, unable to delegate authority or give credit where credit is due. At the time of this session, toward the end of the second year of therapy, the boss had just retired, and Dan was in the process of taking on many of his responsibilities. Dan's father is a retired theologian, but Dan has expressed doubts about how sincere his father's faith is. Dan describes himself as an agnostic, though he is interested in meditation and other New Age philosophies. His general disillusionment with his father as an idealizable selfobject includes his disappointment in his father's ability to offer him spiritual guidance. Much of the time, Dan's father focuses his advice on Dan's career and ignores the state of his soul.

In this particular session Dan begins by describing a phone call with his father in which he is telling him how happy he is at work since the boss retired. His father interrupts to ask if that means he will become the CEO soon. This is something his father has said over the years, and Dan feels injured that his father always holds something higher out rather than give his approval to his present achievement.

Dan begins our discussion in a very controlled way, saying, "I wish I had the presence of mind to say 'That's your fantasy, not mine,' to him." But as he talks about the conversation, Dan gets considerably more agitated and begins to denounce his father. After some time, the energy of this denunciation subsides, and, in describing his father's inability to recognize Dan for who he is, separate from projections, says, "It's the worst thing that ever happened to me."

Sound and rhythm, as we noted in Chapter 1, convey a world of emotional information and open doors to our earliest, implicitly derived memories (Beebe and Lachmann, 2002; Beebe, Cohen, and Lachmann, 2016). Vocal intonation patterns, especially in terms of infant/caregiver matching, are a prime source of the implicit communication that forms the basis of the infant's psychological development (Jaffe et al., 2001).

Here, for purpose of illustration, I have notated the scansion of these two different clusters of statement, as if they were lines of verse, where the "/" represents a stressed syllable and the "U" represents an unstressed one:

```
/  /  U  /  U  /
My father's not a man
  /     /
He's weak
  /  U  /
He's a punk
  /  U  /  U
Hemophilic
  U  /  /  U  /
You touch him he bleeds
```
versus
```
U U   /   /  U  / U  /   U U  /
It's the worst thing that ever happened to me
```

At a glance, one can see the contrast in the predominance of unstressed syllables in the latter statement of lament and the large number of stressed syllables in the former's angrier statements of denunciation. I was struck with the contrast between these two clusters of expression and how they each represented contrasting responses to the oedipal situation: one a world of Dan's anger and his wish to mock his father and be the oedipal victor, the other one of the disappointment and grief of the oedipal victim forever longing for what Kohut (1984) called "the gleam in his father's eye."

I considered, in a moment of silence, a number of possibilities of how to respond to this material. I was tempted to respond to the obviously deep world of feeling expressed in the "worst thing" comment, and my heart was tugged in this direction. Or I could have interpreted the dichotomy of the two responses and tried to bring out the inner conflict they represented. But I was pulled by the energy and music of the angry comments. Somehow I felt that that was what to go with. Perhaps in the moment, it was an aesthetic decision, analogous to the way the poet tries to keep the energy alive in his poem. The angry statements seemed to me to be the "forward edge" of the transference that Marion Tolpin (2002) describes as the "shy tendrils" of a new self-organization, yearning for mirroring and approval.

In the end I said, "'He's a punk. You touch him and he bleeds.' There's a lot of energy behind those statements." A decision whose origins were complex and overdetermined. My own history may have played a part – my father died suddenly when I was 15, denying me the opportunity for an adolescent oedipal struggle I unconsciously may still long for. In any given hour, I might have a preference for anger over grief based on my own mental state or the unconscious content of my reverie. Or I may, as I now think, have been making a quasi-aesthetic choice akin to the making of a poem.

In any event, I sensed a relief in Dan when I approvingly repeated his words. It is as if we were saying together that getting caught in the old grief was not the way to go. Dan's next associations took him to describing an office flirtation he was having. He seemed to enjoy portraying himself as a bit of a ladies' man, even though he was married. In the transference/countertransference field between analyst and patient, something new was emerging, a willingness to seek from me, through his story of office eroticism, the "gleam in his father's eye" that Kohut (1984) describes. A transferential seeking of the new rather than a repetition of the old (Stern, 2017).

Comparing analytic and poetic decision making

The therapist responds to his patient, the poet responds to the emergence of a phrase, an idea for a poem. Both require a series of instant choices. Take too much time in responding to a patient and the moment could be lost, or worse, a message of displeasure or rejection could be conveyed. Take too much time responding to a fragment or poem idea and the impatient muse may move on. Underlying these decisions is a single, controlling intention: to create a work of art or to foster the patient's increased mental health.

Guided by his intention to help the patient, the analyst makes the fundamental choice between silence or comment, and then if he's to comment, on what? The poet faces similar choices. Silence, as we will see in our examination of the work of Paul Celan in Chapter 5, can be conveyed with white space on the page. Poetry can be as noisy as a Blake epic or as quiet as a Dickinson quatrain.

Two spontaneous gestures: "We are approaching God as an asymptote." "My father's not a man. He's weak." The poet chooses to interrogate his material rationally – "What does this statement mean?" – and to do research to support that interrogation. He seeks to find out what the word asymptote means in mathematics, then examines the philosophical implications of this mathematical metaphor.

In the therapist's case, this interrogation happens implicitly and with much more rapidity. His rational process, in approaching a patient like Dan, might be to review his psychoanalytic understanding of men and their fathers. Half-digested bits of Freud, Kohut's reframing of oedipal rivalry into selfobject longing. Who am I, he wonders, in this patient's imagination? Should I help him grieve a loss or provide a developmentally longed-for emotional experience? Could these questions in fact be framed aesthetically? What is the more elegant, the more concise, the more uplifting response?

And moreover, does the act of *thinking*, of choosing a response rather than just responding, obscure our poetic and therapeutic intuition, our implicitly based responsiveness? After his philosophical studies, the poet manages to allow chance (the cartoons) and associations (the neighbor) to shape his poem. Like a horse trainer, he gives the poem its head. Like a good therapist as well.

In contemporary psychoanalysis, as in contemporary poetry, there are few, if any, rules. I am not, unless I choose to be, governed by traditional poetic forms, nor am I in therapy governed by rules such as the need for abstinence. My choice to abstain from comment with Dan for a few beats was more aesthetic than technical. Though MFA training programs and analytic institutes offer much discussion of technique, I think what they offer amounts to what musicians learn through hours of practice: a mastering of chops so you can forget them in performance.

A central act of compositional intention came when, as a poet, I decided to insert the line, "We are approaching God as an asymptote" without comment or context in the middle of the poem. The poet's intention, which was to write a poem containing that line, led him to make (accompanied by much trial and error) an aesthetic decision to let the line stand alone. Behind this decision was a sense that after the poignant story of the neighbor, the poem was backing up and catching its breath, perhaps resetting itself. There was a similar moment in the session with Dan, which also seemed to pause a moment after his outburst to catch its breath.

Poets must learn to make such aesthetic decisions rapidly, so the energy of the work is not lost in indecision, but they also have the luxury of going back and revising. To some extent, wrong or even injurious interpretations can be corrected as well, though it would seem the stakes are higher. Indeed, similar to the revision process of a poem, the attempt on the part of analyst and patient to go back and get it right can be a very meaningful part of the work.

Teachers of creative writing workshops often speak of following the energy or flow of a poem, making comments such as "The energy kind of ebbs right here." It does seem, in retrospect, that the interpretive decision I made with Dan had something to do with following the more energetic angry statements rather than the sadder statement of the catastrophe of his father's disinterest. A poet's ear is, by long training, attuned to following the energy in language, along with the affective music it conveys.

Nonetheless, compositional decisions that lead up to the making of the poem are not the equivalent of the poem itself, which, if successful, takes on a life of its own and surprises even the poet with its eventual form. Similarly, the analytic decisions made in the session with Dan do not "explain" what happened in the session. The emergence of Dan's story of his workplace flirtation was new and unexpected.

While not making any special claims for the "poetic" nature of Dan's treatment, it is possible that my long practice of both shaping and surrendering in the writing of poems created the right ambient mix of openness and authority that allowed Dan to risk making a bid at the end of the session for a fatherly response that would delight in rather than crush his newfound male pride.

When a poet has finished a poem, he can, in effect, hold it up to the light, examine it from all sides. He can share it with friends; he can publish it, God willing, in magazines or a book. No aesthetic object emerges from the therapy process. Nothing one can point to or hold up for very long. To hold too long on any one moment of conjunction, any one interpretation, is to risk dropping out of the process, losing the flow. Therapy requires a willingness to forego narcissistic gratification. The analyst's pride in his craft must perforce be more muted than the poet's, though such pride, found in the scant minutes of reflection between scheduled hours, may help keep us going.

Chapter 3

Near the source of love was this

Poems of the nursery

Let me begin this chapter with some poems about young children and their caretakers:

> It won't be long.
> No, it won't be long.
> There is a melancholy
> in the undersong:
>
> Sweet child
> asleep in your cot,
> little seed head
> there is time yet.
> > (Eavan Boland,
> > "Before Spring,"
> > 2008, p. 93)

> He squeezes his eyes tight
> to hide
> and blink! he's still here.
> It's always a surprise.
>
> Safety-fat,
> angel-fat,
>
> steal it in mouthfuls,
> store it away
> where you save

the face that you touched
for the last time
over and over,
your eyes closed
so it wouldn't go away.
    (Chana Bloch, "Eating
        Babies," 2015, p. 68)

Sweet moans, dovelike sighs
Chase not slumber from thy eyes
Sweet moans, sweeter smiles
All the dovelike moans beguiles

Sleep, sleep, happy child,
All creation slept and smil'd;
Sleep, sleep, happy sleep,
While o'er thee thy mother weep.
        (William Blake, "A Cradle
            Song," 1970, pp. 11–12)

My sleepy son extends his arm up
and pulls my head to his gently breathing chest.
I am floating on his hushed exhalations,
on the call and response of the neighborhood dogs,
the muffled sigh of a returning jetliner.

A curious reversal, a father lying
on his young son's chest as night comes on,
thinking *Everything that holds me is empty*
and later, at the edge of sleep, *If not*
for this love I would fall into space forever.
        (David Shaddock, "Empty," 1997, p. 44)

In this chapter, we will look at what light these and other poems about parents and children may shed on psychoanalytic treatment. The "language" of attachment is the body, a language of gaze, of touch, of movement and gesture. Between the infant and the caregiver, each with 84 face muscles (Ekman, 2003) firing, tugging, relaxing, carrying on a never-ending relay of affects. The two faces are rarely synchronized. The mother appears where the baby thinks she is going to be. The baby leads, the mother follows. The analogous arts are dance and music, not, or not precisely, poetry. The mother and baby solo, they come back to the tonic, they touch and twirl away and touch some more; it culminates in a lift of rapture.

We talk of mirroring between mother and baby, between sympathetic neural networks, but the mirror is a poor metaphor, its only creative act a reversal of left and right. The self emerges from improvisation, not rote repetition. The mother and baby are prisms, sending beams of light in every direction, including back at each other. The mother and baby exist only in the beams of this refraction, their black and white colorized.

The dance of the poem between voice and ear or page and eye mimes this duet, if imprecisely. The poem is gray, inert without the reader. And the reader comes to life with the poem, running ahead, slipping away, doubling back. The poem, in turn, surprises, it enjambs, runs on, jump-cuts to another thought, another image. We nod to the poem we understand, but we fall in love, return again and again, to the poem we can't quite know. "Heavenly hurt it gives us," writes Emily Dickinson (1960, p. 118), and, however painfully, we come into ourselves in the interstices of her words. How we love to let the poem, with its attendant "imperial affliction," run through our fingers.

Heavenly hurt pervades the nursery as well, as the poems at the beginning of this chapter attest. The nursery is a zone out of time, a seed-time, a time under the earth, where the infant's developing self germinates. The caregiver delights in the world out of time, but there is also a note of sadness, for she and the baby are not, in fact, out of time, though only she knows this: "There is melancholy/in the undersong"; a mother touches the baby's face, "over and over/your eyes closed//so it won't go away"; the mother in Blake weeps over her sleeping child; in my own poem a father thinks "as night comes on" that "Everything that holds me is empty."

Though our science of observation and inference has allowed much greater access to the infant's mind, when we turn to poems of infancy and childhood, we find them tracking the parent's mind, not the child's, illuminating what Winnicott (1956) called the Primary Maternal Preoccupation, or what Daniel Stern (1995) calls the Motherhood Constellation. And in these parental minds, anxiety about the future and a foreknowledge of both the child's and the parent's eventual death exist side by side with delight. This knowledge both creates and shapes parental love.

Jacques Lacan (1991) describes this preexisting crack in our psyche – between self and other, between self and the world – as the factor that makes the regulation of self difficult. As if, Lacan implies, we must try to bracket out this crack in our psyche to survive. The caregiver lives in the world of time and loss, trying to forestall the inevitable entry of the infant into that reality by assuring herself, as in the Boland poem, that "there is time yet," or, more graphically, by having a fantasy of "Eating Babies" in the Bloch, to keep them from entering time and "going away."

This note of sadness or anxiety on the part of the caregiver keeps her perpetually just a half beat ahead of the infant, at times anticipating their dysphoria, at other times overreacting. The baby frowns, the mother moves in too close, the baby, frightened by the mother's fright, looks away to avoid overstimulation (Beebe, Cohen, and Lachmann, 2016). The mother wakes from her worried preoccupation, notices the baby and approaches, perhaps a bit cautiously, coos a bit; the baby looks up; a repair is engineered. This pattern of disruption and repair, according to Beebe and Lachmann (2002), is one of the building blocks of the self; it leads the infant to a world in which he can trust others and also trust his own ability to cope with disturbances.

The caregiver's foreknowledge of grief is thus an engine of the infant's development. As Peter Fonagy (Fonagy et al., 2002) points out, the infant's development of the capacity to mentalize, to know the mind of another (and, by extension, his own mind) is fostered by a mix of what he calls *natural/realistic* and *marked/contingent* mirroring. Decoding the communication of the speaker in Bloch's "Eating Babies" requires the infant to absorb the "You're so cute" part – the marked contingent component – as well as the natural/realistic "I want to eat you up." Hopefully while noting, in a nontraumatizing way, the slight (and perhaps even interesting) note of aggression in the latter.

For the modern sensibility, as we see in the Bloch poem, the difference between the child's mind and the mother's mind both ironizes and sanctifies the nursery. This is already evident in Blake, writing 200 years earlier, for whom the mother's tears and the infant's sighs foreshadow a move from "Innocence" to "Experience." As Northrup Frye (1990b) has pointed out, a note of irony pervades the *Songs of Innocence* as the reader scans the often naïve state of the speaker from his perch in the world of experience. And the fallen state of Experience is actually, for Blake, a necessary way station on the road to higher consciousness. The caregiver and baby are reenacting *felix culpa*, the fortunate (or at least necessary) fall.

Here Dawn McGuire, on the occasion of her now-adult son's stifled cry on the phone, chronicles another dimension of this fall, the movement of consciousness from the body into language:

> The word *body* enters the body
> converts its substance
>
> swallows its air. Pitch and silence
> define the body now.
>
> Slick reticular switchbacks
> convey what you say.
>
> Diverticular crypts
> hide what you hide.
>
> When my son suckled
> he hummed. When hungry he cried.
>
> Where is my body's endless milk?
> Its wordless fleece?
>
> Tonight, hand over mouthpiece,
> stifled, his cry.
>   (McGuire, "Everything
>   About the Subject," 2017)

Since we are discussing a move from the nonverbal to the verbal domain, let us take a moment to listen to the nonverbal elements in the poems we are examining, at how these poems note the shift from the open and inviting sounds of "my body's endless milk" to "slick reticular switchbacks" and "diverticular crypts." As we saw in Chapter 2, patients' speech rhythms often reflect this mix of chopped, angular sounds and longer, more open ones through which the feeling pours in. The longer vowels of "little seed-head" yield to the more staccato "there is time yet" at the end of the Boland poem. Or in Blake's heartbreaking rhyme, sleep/weep.

The idea that the difference in subjectivity between the mother and the baby might lead to different vocal rhythms or intonations leads to another topic in child development. Beatrice Beebe and her colleagues (Jaffe et al.,

2001) found, in their study of mother/infant vocal coordination, that too close coordination in vocal intonation between mother and baby predicted insecure attachment, as did too loose a coordination. Best to have, Beebe maintains, a midrange of coordination, which she compares (Beebe and McRorie, 1996) to improvised jazz, with both mother and baby free to improvise away from the "theme" but coming back to it again and again. Beebe has pointed out that in birdsong, when one bird imitates the other's song note for note, it is a territorial challenge. So the mix of long/short tonal effects we find in some of these nursery poems might point the way to the nature of a developmentally enhancing intersubjective dialog, one that is generalizable to the clinical situation.

We must keep also in mind that the caregiver/child dyad is a two-person system. It is not just the parent's knowledge of the world outside that disrupts the apparent oneness of the nursery. That would ignore what we now know about infants: they are intelligent, curious, furious agents of their own destiny at birth, and probably before. And ultimately, God willing, they will outlive us. Here is a wonderful poem by George Oppen that gets at some of this:

> . . . Lying in her father's arms, the little seed eyes
> Moving, trying to see, smiling for us. . . .
> To see, she will make a household
> To her need of these rooms – Sara, little seed,
> Little violent, diligent seed. Come let us look at the world
> Glittering: this seed will speak,
> Max, words! There will be no other words in the world
> But those our children speak
>   ("Sara in Her Father's Arms," 2002, p. 51)

We catch our babies in midair; we delight in them; we curtail them with our worry; they pass us and supplant us. There will be no other words in the world than theirs someday. Oppen imagines a generational life cycle: from wordless "seed" (used three times: again that word, all potential, all possibility, as in the Boland poem), wholly dependent on the words her father speaks for her representation in language, to having her own words and inhabiting a world she makes more and more with her own language, to leaving her father's language completely behind and becoming, in Wallace Stevens's words, the "the single artificer of the world" (1978, p. 128). Our language separates us from our infants; their language eventually separates them from us.

Another aspect of the gap in subjectivity between parent and child is the parent's sense of her own flaws and her desire not to pass them along. Here's Yeats in "A Prayer for My Daughter":

> My mind, because the minds that I have loved
> The sort of beauty that I have approved
> Prosper but little, has dried up of late,
> Yet knows that to be choked with hate
> May well be of all evil chances chief.
>
> . . .
>
> Considering that, all hatred's driven hence
> The soul recovers radical innocence
> And learns at last that it is self-delighting
> Self-appeasing, self-affrighting,
> And that its own sweet will is Heaven's will;
> She can, though every face should scowl
> Or every windy quarter howl
> Or every bellows burst, be happy still.
>
> (1996, p. 188)

Revealingly, the poet wishes that his daughter occupy a state of "radical innocence" in which her soul can learn to be "self-delighting/ Self-appeasing, self-affrighting." His own subjectivity controlled by disappointment in others, the poet wishes for his daughter a preference for self-soothing over the interactive. Free from the disappointments of face-to-face regulation, "though every face should scowl," his daughter can "be happy still." Of course, this poem reveals more of Yeats's mind than his daughter's. His prayer is that she should not be unhappy like him.

The transmission of trauma

In Yeats's poem the unhappy parent says, in effect, don't be like me. But in traumatogenic parent/child dyads, the parent says, consciously or unconsciously, "Do be like me, do suffer because I suffer." Here are two passages, from vastly different eras, in which the parents inflict their own unhappiness on their children:

The Clasp

She was four, he was one, it was raining, we had colds,
we had been in the apartment two weeks straight,
I grabbed her to keep her from shoving him over on his
face, again, and when I had her wrist
in my grasp I compressed it, fiercely, for a couple
of seconds, to make an impression on her,
to hurt her, our beloved firstborn, I even almost
savored the stinging sensation of the squeezing,
the expression, into her, of my anger,
"Never, never, again," the righteous
chant accompanying the clasp. It happened very
fast-grab, crush, crush,
crush, release – and at the first extra
force, she swung her head, as if checking
who this was, and looked at me,
and saw me – yes, this was her mom,
her mom was doing this. Her dark,
deeply open eyes took me
in, she knew me, in the shock of the moment
she learned me. This was her mother, one of the
two whom she most loved, the two
who loved her most, near the source of love
was this.

(Olds, "The Clasp," 2012, p. 161)

Medea. . . . Come pick up the sword,
Wretched hand of mine. Pick up the sword,
Move to where your life of misery begins.
Don't play the coward. Don't remember now
How much you love them, how you gave them life.
For this short day forget they are your children
And mourn them later. Although you kill them,
Still you loved them. As a woman, I'm so sad.

(Euripides, *Medea*, 2005, 1243–1250)

In these two extraordinary passages, we enter into a maternal world in which love and cruelty intertwine. One does not cancel the other; they coexist in a swirling complexity.

In the research of Mary Main and Erik Hesse (1990), the conflating of love, terror and anger runs as self-replicating patterns through traumatized mothers and their disorganized-attachment-prone children. Maternal trauma seems to be the leading predictor of attachment derailment. In Olds's poem, a stressed-out mother on a rainy day crosses a boundary into cruelty, and clearly, chillingly and yes, with a kind of compassion, registers her daughter's confusion. A maternal look that is both frightened and frightening can lie at the base of a child's disorganization write Main and Hesse. When this is the case, the child can only turn for comfort to the very one who hurts and frightens him. Olds's poem chronicles the daughter's loss of innocence: "I even almost savored the stinging sensation of the squeezing," the sibilants piling up, like a hissing snake. There is a kind of yielding, as if to a dark power, but that power doesn't vanquish love.

Likewise, Medea, in her dissociated-seeming state, about to murder her own children, is not oblivious to the consequences of her act. She feels maternal love. She knows that she is only delaying an overwhelming feeling of guilt and grief. Yet she pushes herself onward, decries any urges to stop her horrible plan as cowardice.

Implicitly, we suspect that beneath these isolated fragments, a history of a mother's own trauma lurks. There is no backstory given in the short Olds poem. But those familiar with her work would know that she has written about childhood experiences of abuse and dysfunction. And of course we know of Medea's betrayal by Jason. Can these portraits instill compassion for mothers, as well as for their damaged offspring?

But these are poems, recreations, reflections on the mothers' mental state. They are not documentaries or legal documents in some court case. In this, they resemble the situation in our office when a patient who is a parent reflects on her interactions with a child. The distinctions, differences and disturbances these poets mark between themselves and their children all flow from the primary fault we noted at the beginning of this chapter between babies and their caregivers, albeit here in terrible, tragic ways. When we are listening to a parent in our office, it is tempting to leap across this fault and let our sympathy drift toward the child. But as the following vignette shows, for a parent with a trauma history, such a lapse, however momentary, can be retraumatizing.

Case vignette

When we treat a parent in individual therapy, we have, effectively, three generations in our consulting room: therapist, patient and patient's child. Each illuminates the other, and each casts its shadow.

Stephanie, a mother in her early 40s, had two children with complex, genetically derived disabilities. Because of a history of abuse by her mother, she was determined to break the cycle and protect, not harm, her children. But at times, it seemed to me, her fierce desire to protect and stand up for her children interfered with her ability to simply mother them. The division between empathically immersing myself in the world of trauma that lay behind Stephanie's parenting commitment and my imagination of her children's experience in some ways resembled the split in consciousness between parent and infant documented by the poets at the beginning of this chapter.

Stephanie's mother apparently suffered from a complex dissociative disorder. Throughout Stephanie's childhood, she would be unbearably cruel and abusive and then sweet and rather ineffectual, depending on which of her subpersonalities was active. She would frequently wake Stephanie in the middle of the night, berate her for being stupid, sometimes physically attack her as well; she would force her to get up and assign her to do extra homework on the spot. A constant and chilling refrain was her telling her daughter she should have aborted her. Her father, a physician, was dedicated to his patients but oblivious to the disorder in his own house.

At a certain point in our work, Stephanie became embroiled in a fight with her older son's school over their adherence to a Special Education Plan. When the school district offered a to-me-reasonable-sounding resolution, I – thinking accepting it would free her up to concentrate more on her son's needs than on the fight with the school district – urged her to accept it. What I failed to see was that, because of her trauma, she had in the moment only limited ability to separate her own subjective experience from her child's. She must protect her child-self/child at all costs.

The arc between a mother like the one in Bloch's poem fantasizing eating her baby and Medea (or Stephanie's mother) actually taking a bite marks a collapse of an enlivening space into a traumatogenic one. Consciously or not, the abusive parent cannot bear or protect the child's innocence. The speaker in the Olds poem forces her knowledge of the pain of the world onto her four-year-old. Likewise for Stephanie, her fall into the world of experience was traumatically induced. Her mother could not bear the reality that she was a sweet child and a good student. My forcing my complex understanding of her problem with the school district on her parent-self reenacted that trauma. She was too young therapeutically for the insertion of my other-centered opinion. I needed to merely empathically note the difference between our two subjective points of view.

The result was a disruption of our until-then-smoothly-unfolding treatment. What I said reflected an understandable concern for her son. But it amounted to a betrayal of our therapeutic alliance and a potential retraumatization. To try and repair this rupture, which was evident by her unusually subdued tone in our next session, I took a risk of self-disclosure. I told her that years ago I had been in a fight with a school district over my own son's Special Education Plan, and that I had allowed myself to assume, without explaining where I was coming from, that my successful resolution of that dispute might be a useful model for her. This, I admitted, was a mistake in my thinking, the situations weren't that analogous, and I had forgotten for a moment what abandoning her son to an imperfect situation would mean to her. This made a bit of an impact and started a cycle of repair, but the real repair was the silent commitment I made to appreciate rather than obliterate the gap between our two subjectivities.

The vignette illuminates the way the shifting figure/ground relationship between the parent's immersion in the child's world and her own adult subjectivity can be replicated in a therapeutic relationship. We parent/therapists have, with our clinical acumen, a knowledge of the world our patients do not possess, just as they, bounded in their own subjectivity, live in a world we can never really know. In the nursery, as in our consulting room, the gap can be filled with the fantasy of where the "little seed head" might be headed. A fantasy filled with love but tinged with a bit of sadness: "soon there will be no other words in the world but hers." Or it can be filled with disjuncture and a breakdown in the empathic connection. The poets do us a great service to chronicle the vicissitudes of their own parenting experience, particularly those terrible moments when the gap between innocence and experience becomes unbearable.

Chapter 4

Standing against silence

Czeslaw Milosz, Denise Levertov and poetry of witness

> What then can exist between the scream and the silence?
> (Sam Gerson, "When the Third Is Dead," 2009)

> It is possible that there is no other memory than the memory of wounds.
> (Czeslaw Milosz, "The Nobel Lecture," 1981)

A woman of 45 comes into my office looking troubled. She's been haunted of late by childhood memories that seem indistinct. She describes a recent visit from her father, whom she usually finds kind and support-ive. But something about his blue eyes, the way they seem permanently amused, has caught her attention. Then she locates the memory: "That's the way he used to look all the time, even after my mother would have one of her fits." (She has been remembering how her nearly psychotic mother would go into violently abusive and incoherent rages.) The mem-ory of those eyes with their discordant affect now fills her with anger and sadness. "He should have protected us children rather than just be happy all the time."

Traumatic memories live in details like the image of those eyes. When poets bear witness to trauma, it is those details they capture and focus on. The way poets have borne witness to trauma, both historical and personal, can instruct the way therapists bear such witness. As the poems we will examine here demonstrate, part of the witness such poems bear is to the poet's own helplessness in the face of such horror, either to intervene or to adequately bear witness. Such acknowledgment of limitation is instructive to us as therapists.

In 1943, during the burning of the Warsaw Ghetto, Czeslaw Milosz writes of the contrast between ordinary life in Warsaw, which continued obliviously, and the Holocaust nearby:

> At times wind from the burning
> would drift dark kites along
> and riders on the carousel
> caught petals in midair . . .
>   (Milosz, "Campo dei
>   Fiori," 2001, p. 33)

But for

> Those dying here, the lonely
> forgotten by the world,
> our tongue becomes for them
> the language of an ancient planet . . .
>   (pp. 34–35)

The ancient planet is the one where grief and trauma are registered, not this planet where the abused child goes to school, where she hears the other children playing on the playground, oblivious, just like the revelers in Warsaw, to the trauma that sets her inexorably apart. Traumatized people live in a separate world (Stolorow, 2007), one known to the rest of the world only by smoke on the horizon. The poet, like the analyst, must heal the split between daily life and trauma, must be a bridge between the quotidian, which in the context of trauma takes on a shade of the ominous, and the sequestered trauma.

The poem is what Thomas Ogden (2004) and other contemporary psychoanalysts refer to as the *third*; it emerges as a new term between the poet's witnessing and the world's sorrow. Milosz writes of the craft behind his poetry of witness in his introduction to his *New and Collected Poems* (2001):

> The history of the twentieth century prompted many poets to design images that conveyed their moral protest. Yet to remain aware of the weight of the fact without yielding to the temptation to become only a

reporter is one of the most difficult puzzles confronting a practitioner of poetry. It calls for a cunning in selecting one's means and a kind of distillation of material to achieve a distance to contemplate the things of the world as they are, without illusion.

(p. xxiii)

It is valuable for therapists to look closely at Milosz's "cunning," his strategies for presenting a world without illusions. One key is his use of the irony of natural juxtapositions. He will find the telling detail, the image that will carry a narrative, just as the image of my patient's father's blue eyes carries her narrative to a place beyond denotation. He will then juxtapose that detail with an observation of the ongoingness of the world. Notice the masterful details in "A Treatise on Poetry: III. The Spirit of History":

> Chickens cackle. Geese stretch their necks from baskets.
> In the town, a bullet is carving a dry trace
> In the sidewalk near bags of homegrown tobacco.
> All night long, on the outskirts of the city,
> An old Jew, tossed in a clay pit, has been dying.
> His moans subside only when the sun comes up.
> The vistula is gray, it washes through osiers
> And fashions fans of gravel in the shallows.
>
> (2001, p. 127)

Farm animals and an old man dying a death of unimaginable cruelty. Bullets and a new cash crop. Sunrise and the death of a tortured Jew. The fans of alluvial gravel at the river verge. We cannot begin to understand our patient's traumatic experience unless we understand its context – the families that contained or allowed it, the world that, just by going on being, failed to witness their experience. This goes beyond what Hannah Arendt termed "the banality of evil." The details in this poem indict: the context is complicit.

That is what my patient was trying to tell me with her story of her father's smile and his blue eyes. The context is complicit. My patient rages at her husband, a decent if somewhat unimaginative man. She rages at me as I try to interpret her family history. But Milosz's poetry helps me understand – I am complicit. If I say we have to stop now, if I start a session with small talk, if I get out in front of her and push my understanding. The gravel fan of the vistula, the statue on my desk of a wolf howling at the moon; Milosz bids me understand that it is all complicit, even the sun, dawning on a new day as the old man perishes in a clay pit.

The witness function in therapy

In a normally functioning dyadic system (Beebe and Lachmann, 2014), be it parent/caregiver or therapist/patient, a sense of *we*-ness emerges that comes to encompass and organize the dyad. In systems parlance, the two individual subjectivities become part of a supersystem. The use of the term the *third* in recent psychoanalytic discourse gets at some of this same thinking. This "third" is essential for psychic functioning, it provides a space for development to move into, and it holds the psyche in a larger container. Gerson (2009) describes this third as "the other through whom life gestates and into whom futures are born." He identifies three types of this third: the developmental, which we are just describing; the relational, an extension of this concept to all intersubjective relationships; and the cultural, which gets at the way cultural institutions foster (or fail to foster) individual security and development. This latter, according to Gerson, involves "the existence and impact of all the non-personal contexts and processes within which each individual lives and that shapes the nature of their development" (p. 1342). Gerson, in his evocatively named paper "When the Third Is Dead," names these three essential functions to highlight what happens in cases of extreme trauma, such as genocide, when developmental, interpersonal and cultural contexts all fail to function.

It is then we need a witness, an outside actor that can restore the necessary psychic space for us to function. In this chapter, we will explore the way a poetry of witness can both restore the "cultural third" by bearing collective witness to trauma, with the hope that it will guide the interpersonal therapy process with trauma survivors. We will look in detail at two poems, "Dedication" by Czeslaw Milosz and "Advent 1966" by Denise Levertov.

The act of witness, of evoking a third, is more complex than a self-object experience, such as mirroring. It is more than saying "that must have been awful" or "how terrified and alone you must've felt." That type of response assumes the existence of a living third, which is evoked by accurate attunement (Gerson, 2009). A witness must perforce be another, a subjectivity that exists outside the trauma space. We shall see this when we discuss the work of Czeslaw Milosz, who felt that a poetry of witness could only be achieved by achieving a distance, a "soaring above." But, as he maintained at his Nobel Prize lecture, this distancing implicated him in a kind of "moral treason" (1981). To insist on one's separate subjectivity is a kind of treason. But in contrast to mere documentary reporting, it is the only way the act of witnessing can constitute a living third.

This is what Carolyn Forché (1993) is getting at when she describes a poem of witness as a new, separate trauma. Following the thought of Walter Benjamin, Forché writes,

> a poem is *itself* an event, a trauma, that changes both a common language and an individual psyche, it is a specific kind of event, a specific kind of trauma. It is an experience entered into voluntarily. Unlike an aerial attack, a poem does not come at one unexpectedly. One has to read or listen, one has to be willing to accept the trauma. So, if a poem is an event and the trace of an event, it has, by definition, to belong to a different order of being from the trauma that marked its language in the first place.
>
> (p. 33)

It is our hope that the trauma of such a poem can somehow heal – or at least cauterize – the original trauma.

Let me now bring in the voice of Sam Gerson (2009) whose magnificent paper, "When the Third Is Dead: Memory, Mourning, and Witnessing in the Aftermath of the Holocaust," underlies much of my thinking in this chapter. Expanding the quotation that serves as an epigraph for this chapter, Gerson writes,

> What then can exist between the scream and the silence? We hope first that there is a witness – an other that stands beside the event and the self and who cares to listen, an other who is able to contain that which is heard and is capable of imagining the unbearable; an other who is in a position to confirm both our external and our psychic realities and, thereby, to help us integrate and live within all realms of our experience. This is the presence that lives in the gap, absorbs absence, and transforms our relation to loss. This is the third – between the experience and its meaning, between the real and the symbolic, is the other through whom life gestates and into whom futures are born.
>
> (p. 1342)

The poets we discuss in this chapter, Denise Levertov and Czeslaw Milosz, both make a conscious and moral choice to create art that will constitute this third. As part of that process, they include their own subjectivity, which includes their experience of the near-impossibility of the task and of the toll it takes on the artist's psyche.

The events our two poets describe, the Holocaust and World War II in Europe and the Napalm carpet-bombing of Vietnam, are so pervasive and traumatogenic that the act of witness simultaneously bears witness to the crushing of the possibility of witness. The poems acknowledge the collapse of the existing cultural third: the ongoing European community that Milosz, now an exile himself, once belonged to; or the consoling Christian religion evoked by the Christmas season and Levertov's recalling of Southwell's resurrection poem, "The Burning Babe."

Here is Gerson (2009) on this condition:

> [I]magine life when the third is dead, when the container cracks and there is no presence beyond our own subjectivity to represent continuity. It is a world constituted by absence where meaning is ephemeral and cynicism passes for wisdom; a world in which psychic numbness is the balm against unbearable affects, where feelings of ennui and emptiness replace guilt and shame, and where manias of all sorts masquerade as Eros. This is the world created by proliferating traumas, injuries not acknowledged or, if recognized, not sufficiently healed before the next blow falls, and, as the next becomes an inevitability, the cascade of assaults forces us either to hide from our fears behind the false security of a 'gated community' or to confront them with the false security of unconscionable force.
>
> (p. 1343)

Let us now turn to a poem written in the midst of World War II and the Holocaust, which simultaneously witnesses the collapse of the third that Gerson describes and, by its very existence, tries to reconstitute it.

Czeslaw Milos: "Dedication"

Czeslaw Milosz (1911–2004) was born in a small village in what is now Lithuania but was then Poland. His parents spoke Polish, but Lithuanian was the language of the street around him. He survived the war in Warsaw unscathed, at least physically, save for one incident of narrowly escaping capture by the Nazis. He witnessed many atrocities during the war, including the destruction of the Warsaw Ghetto. After the war, he worked as a cultural attaché for the communist government before he escaped to exile, first in Paris and then in Berkeley. He won the Nobel Prize for Literature in 1980.

Milosz's poems are often situated between spiritual longing and material realism. The poem "Dedication" chronicles both his sense of duty to report from the traumatized world and his longing to be free of that duty.

Dedication

You whom I could not save
Listen to me.
Try to understand this simple speech as I would be ashamed of another.
I swear, there is in me no wizardry of words.
I speak to you with silence like a cloud or a tree.

What strengthened me, for you was lethal.
You mixed up farewell to an epoch with the beginning of a new one,
Inspiration of hatred with lyrical beauty,
Blind force with accomplished shape.

Here is the valley of shallow Polish rivers. And an immense bridge
Going into white fog. Here is a broken city,
And the wind throws the screams of gulls on your grave
When I am talking with you.

What is poetry which does not save
Nations or people?
A connivance with official lies,
A song of drunkards whose throats will be cut in a moment,
Readings for sophomore girls.
That I wanted good poetry without knowing it,
That I discovered, late, its salutary aim,
In this and only this I find salvation.

They used to pour millet on graves or poppy seeds
To feed the dead who would come disguised as birds.

I put this book here for you, who once lived
So that you should visit us no more.

(pp. 78–79)

The Milosz translator and scholar Peter Dale Scott (2017) has written that Milosz later renounced or at least felt ambivalent about this poem's bold statement that poetry that does not save people is either treasonous or trivial. Still, the poem, written in 1945, stands as a valid depiction of the poet's state of mind at the time.

The poem breaks into three parts: a direct address to the dead, a meditation on poetry and a spell against haunting. Each represents a different state of the author's mind in relation to the trauma of the war. It is this chronicling of the witness's mind, which we will find also in the Levertov poem, that I wish to emphasize. The witness must also bear witness to the trauma and dislocation that the act of witnessing entails. Without this, there can be no third, just a joining of one on one. This inclusion of the author's subjectivity could be an example of subtle narcissism: "look how terrific I am to be writing about this terrible subject." And perhaps in the hands of a lesser artist, that would be the case. But here we have the creation of a poem that is, in Forché's (1993) description, a second trauma, a kind of counter-trauma.

The opening lines, with their faint echo of the gladiatorial salute – "we who are about to die" – strike the note of melancholy and irony that will sound throughout the poem. "Listen to me," but of course they can't. Like Prospero in *The Tempest*, the poet renounces his wizardry. He has no literary magic, no grand resurrective plan to offer the dead and traumatized. Only the silence of a cloud or a tree. We will see this same renouncing of the resurrective in Levertov's "Advent 1966," when she compares her vision of napalmed infants to Southwell's 16th-century Christmas poem "The Burning Babe." Worse, the author notes, "what strengthened me," e.g., poetry and the life of imagination, "was lethal for you," presumably because of the people's romance with the idealism of fascism or communism. Though I wonder how this applies to the majority of Poles who were victims of, not players in, history.

"Dedication's" third stanza, "Here is the valley of shallow Polish rivers . . ." with its naturalism and elegiac tone, stands at the heart of the poem. A landscape: "Bridge with Gulls and Broken City." The other side of the bridge shrouded in fog, the most this poem against the hubris of poetry will allow itself of metaphor. Here, as the poet imagines talking to the dead with the sound of the gulls drifting over their graves, his grief surmounts his self-recrimination. But only for a moment.

As if pulling himself from a reverie, Milosz now, with the stanza that begins "What is poetry that does not save/Nations or people," renews his brief against poetry, against the lyric impulse in general. It is survivor's guilt at play here. For even as this seems to be an indictment of bourgeois aestheticism or bland collaboration with evil, the target of this argument is not sophomore girls or literary professors, it is the author himself. Who survived, who found salvation in "good poetry." In his Nobel acceptance speech of 1980, Milosz makes this self-indictment more explicitly: "Reality calls for a name, for words, but it is unbearable, and if it is touched, if it draws very close, the poet's mouth cannot even utter a complaint of Job: all art proves to be nothing compared to action" (1981, quoted in Scott, 2017, pp. 276–277).

All art, all therapy, indeed all witnessing of any kind proves to be nothing compared to action. An action that is forever too late. But what else do we have to offer those who have suffered the unspeakable but an authentic account of our own futility? And a confession such as this one on Milosz's part, of his guilt at finding salvation in poetry while the others perished.

In the remarkable final stanza of this poem, the poet who has just renounced the wizardry of poetry uses poetry to cast a spell against the haunting of the dead. As Gerson (2009) notes, "the third constituted by ghosts and phantoms leaves us alone in the shadows of destruction" (p. 1349). The poem that the author leaves on the graves instead of millet seed is two things simultaneously. It is a spell against the tug of his own ineffectual guilt, a wish to pry his own witnessing psyche free from the deadness engendered by what he has witnessed. And most profoundly, it is also a spell on behalf of the dead, that they can rest in their graves and haunt the living no more.

We move forward in time some 20 years to another poet, Denise Levertov, and another trauma-inducing war, Vietnam.

Denise Levertov: "Advent 1966"

In her essay "Poetry, Prophecy and Survival" (1992a), Denise Levertov (1923–1997) writes of her twin commitments as a poet to witness the horrors of the world and also to praise its beauty: "If we lose the sense of contrast of the opposites to all the grime and gore, the torture, the banality of the computerized apocalypse, we lose the reason for trying to work for redemptive change" (p. 144). This loss of the praise-urge corresponds to the deadness that severe trauma engenders.

Denise was my teacher and mentor and later a close friend. I learned from her what it meant to be an artist who committed fully to her work and, through that work, to have a passionate commitment to document injustice and work for social change. Her commitment to be "poet in the World" (1992b) informs this book.

She was born outside of London. Her father was a scion of a long line of Hasidic rabbis; following a vision he had as a young man, he himself became an Anglican minister. Her mother came from a line of Welsh mystics. Denise was thus the natural inheritor of three deep traditions, Jewish, Celtic and Christian. A mystical connection to the world, to the radiant sparks that hide in things, to use a Hasidic phrase, informs her earliest work. But horror, and its attendant despair, was never a stranger either. In an early poem of witness, "During the Eichmann Trial" (2013, pp. 173–178), she writes, "there is more blood than/sweet juice/always more blood – ." As a young woman of 19 she worked as a volunteer nurse in London, tending to the victims of the Blitz.

Levertov married the American writer Mitch Goodman after the war, moved to the U.S., met and emulated such writers as William Carlos Williams, Robert Duncan and Robert Creeley, and transformed herself into an American poet. An American poet who defied the fashion for self-confessional poetry and instead wrote passionate, political poems such as the one we are about to examine. In the 80s, as the endless horrors of America's wars of choice wore on, along with a growing concern for the ecological perils the planet faced, Levertov moved from a kind of generalized spirituality to becoming a practicing Catholic and a writer of specifically Christian poetry. I have elsewhere (Shaddock, 2013) offered a more detailed account of this movement.

The poem we will be looking at here, "Advent 1966," was first published in *The Nation* in 1967, before Levertov formally converted to Catholicism, but it demonstrates some of the longings and uncertainties that were behind that conversion. The poem has two distinct movements, one in which the lack of any religious or poetic container to hold the horror she beholds is acknowledged, and the other a phenomenological account of her perception of that horror without such a containing vision.

The poem begins with an acknowledgment of the death of a living cultural third, and its replacement with a kind of mechanized, repetitive numbness:

Advent 1966

Because in Vietnam the vision of a Burning Babe
is multiplied, multiplied,
the flesh on fire
not Christ's, as Southwell saw it, prefiguring
the Passion upon the Eve of Christmas,

but wholly human and repeated, repeated,
infant after infant, their names forgotten,
their sex unknown in the ashes,
set alight, flaming but not vanishing,
not vanishing as his vision but lingering.
                              (Levertov, 2013, pp. 342–343)

The 16th-century Robert Southwell poem Levertov alludes to depicts the same type of suffering but in a completely different system of meanings and allusions. "Lifting up a fearful eye to view what fire was near," in Southwell's (1963, p. 94) vision "A pretty Babe all burning bright did in the air appear;/Who, scorched with excessive heat, such floods of tears did shed/As though his floods should quench his flames which with his tears were fed." But this vision takes place inside a cultural third of transformative Christian iconography, in which it prefigures Christ's resurrective triumph over human suffering. Rather than the suffering of nameless infants, the poem is about Christ's love and innocence, whose "faultless breast the furnace is." Under the sheltering cover of this Christian mythos, the tortured infant prefigures joy. This may be hard, in a secular age, to grasp, but the existence of the third here allows for a potentially traumatic vision to be changed into its opposite.

Levertov, however much she might wish it, is denied a vision of a "unique Holy Infant/burning sublimely, an imagination of redemption" by the mechanized impersonal horror of the Vietnam War. Further, where Milosz could guiltily confess to being "saved" by the imagination, here

Levertov's poetic craft itself fails her. She writes "my clear caressive sight, my poet's sight I was given/that it might stir me to song,/is blurred." The poem continues,

> There is a cataract filming over
> my inner eyes. Or else a monstrous insect
> has entered my head, and looks out
> from my sockets with multiple vision.

We are witness to a kind of Kafkaesque metamorphosis, one that illustrates the Blakean dictum, "He became what he beheld." A miracle of nature, the bee's multifaceted vision, is here transformed into something alien and mechanical, a runaway Xerox machine or errant tape loop, churning out endless iterations of the same horror:

> seeing not the unique Holy Infant
> burning sublimely, an imagination of redemption,
> furnace in which souls are wrought into new life,
> but, as off a beltline, more, more senseless figures aflame.

Levertov's use of the adjective "senseless" here is telling. Where, in a poem like this, one expects a condemnation of "senseless horror," a moral statement, here the word applies to the state of the burned infants, who lack the capacity to sense at all. The poem concludes as a kind of confession of the limits of the poet's ability to adequately witness the horror:

> And this insect (who is not there –
> it is my own eyes do my seeing, the insect
> is not there, what I see is there)
> will not permit me to look elsewhere,
>
> or, if I look, to see except dulled and unfocused
> the delicate, firm whole flesh of the still unburned.

The ending of this poem is complex. Beyond just a record of the effects of the war, the poet wishes to record, as if in antidote to horror, one unburned infant. But her traumatized, insect-like gaze will not, cannot, look away from the images of horror and retrieve a symbol of hope and innocence.

Neither Milosz nor Levertov is offering salvation from a world of trauma. What we find instead is a confession of limitation. Milosz the ironist bids the dead to listen. Levertov is too transfixed by horror to offer a vision of hope, Christian or otherwise. But these are finished poems, not excuses for not writing poems. In their recording of the failure of their capacity to witness or redeem, they offer us their existence as works of art. Both Levertov's "dull unfocused" imagination of a living infant and Milosz's offering of his poem as a kind of spell to quiet the restless dead guide our work as therapists. The humanity we display in admitting what we are both capable and incapable of is all we have to offer the victims of unspeakable trauma. Perhaps, in the truth of that meeting, something redemptive will emerge.

I will end this discussion of Milosz and Levertov with a personal anecdote. At a dinner that Denise and I attended at Milosz's house in Berkeley, Czeslaw began, seemingly out of nowhere, declaiming a poem in Polish. It took a minute, but then Denise exclaimed, "Why Czeslaw, have you been translating my poems?" When he nodded, the two shared a delighted hug. The poem he was reading was "Eyemask" (2013, p. 869), a poem of her spiritual unreadiness, which, in the light of both their acts of poetic witness, can also be read as a prayer for respite: "I need/more of the night before I open . . . I must still/grow in the dark like a root/not ready at all" (p. 869). The poet, and by extension the therapist, must seek her readiness for the work, including the work of witnessing trauma, in her innermost place of darkness and silence.

Case example

"During the day, I knew places I could hide from my mother. But at night, in bed, in the middle of the night, that's when I could not hide." Rae is a 40-year-old woman, but she is shaking like a young child as she tells this. "She would say I hadn't cleaned the kitchen, or vacuumed the living room, and she would insist that I get up and start cleaning in the middle of the night. She'd drag me out of bed by my hair, and if I made the slightest protest, she would start slapping me around. She would hit me and hit me, but she knew enough never to leave marks."

Rae is telling her husband and me this in a couples therapy session, some two years into the treatment. Up until this time, she has been vague, referring only to "those things that happened when I was a child." But now she continued to tell her story. "She would say we were going to go clothes shopping, but she would start in on me, and throw me out of the car, a mile or two from our house. One time a neighbor notified the school but nothing ever happened. My father was a prominent man in our town." Her mother didn't drink or use drugs and often seemed quite normal. Only Rae bore the full weight of the truth about how crazy and abusive she was.

I asked Carey, her husband, if he had heard all of this. "In bits and pieces. But never all put together like this," he replied in a subdued voice.

For months we had been slogging along. Carey had a boyish charm, but try as he might to do the right thing, he always ended up on Rae's bad side. The dishes weren't put in the dishwasher right, the card he thought would be funny wasn't. He was a bad listener, interrupted too much. He wasn't ambitious enough at work, should apply for a different job. Carey spent all his free time tinkering with his bicycles; his time in the basement drove Rae crazy. He shrugged off her complaints until he couldn't any-more, then he would say, "Fine, if you want a divorce, let's get a divorce." Rae would get very angry at first, but then, in the middle of a fight, she would start begging him not to leave. Carey would look to me helplessly, asking, "What am I supposed to do?"

I have written (Shaddock, 2000) about the untapped potential for couples therapy to address issues of developmental deficits and childhood trauma. The couple's relationship is reminiscent of the infant/caregiver dyad, and the three-person couples therapy situation echoes the family. In my work I look for new openings, new possibilities, opportunities to replace the ties that bound with a tie that could heal. This individual growth then redounds into new possibilities, new intimacies in the relationship. But over the course of this treatment, though both partners showed signs of individual growth, the relationship did not change much.

Carey, in particular, seemed to grow in stature and maturity. Early on, he complained about their sex life. Why was she sometimes very passionate, then cold for weeks and months? And why couldn't she at least cuddle, even if she wasn't ready to be intimate? He would deal with this rejection by pursuing sex vigorously for a while then withdraw to his basement workshop even more of the time, barely showing up for meals.

As the story of Rae's abuse became more a part of our conversation, Carey seemed to change. He came to understand that as a child, Rae had had no control over who touched her and when. He began to see his role as that of a protector. They developed a language for her to signal when she could bear to be touched and when she couldn't. And Carey took the lead in maintaining those protocols.

Rae was trying too. She had entered into individual therapy, and her knowledge about her own triggers and her skill at handling them by herself grew. But she would still find herself railing at Carey, unable to stop. Their sex life did not really improve except in rare times of renewed passion. And the sense that something was missing, some rapport and liveliness that other couples seemed to have, did not change.

In one session, after about two years of treatment, Carey came in very discouraged. He said he was ready to give up. Not leave; he still loved Rae. But give up trying to do better, to improve things. I said, almost surprising myself, that I had been having a similar thought. I cared deeply for them, felt committed to both of them as individuals and to their relationship, but I didn't think I could do much more to help them. The room was silent for quite a while. I worried that Rae might read this as both of us dismissing her, telling her she was damaged goods. But her face was still and open, a few tears running down her cheek. Perhaps, I thought, this is what she needed all along. Our admission of failure and impotence was an affective bridge into her world, where everything felt like that. In admitting our hopelessness, we were, in the only way possible, witnessing that what had happened to her was real, was unimaginably devastating.

This is a bit of what the poems of Milosz and Levertov are saying. "I could not save you." "My dulled unfocussed vision." Take this poem, this scrap of seed. Perhaps it will still these restless ghosts, these legacies of trauma begetting trauma. That the still unburned, at least, may flourish.

Chapter 5

Knowing the unknowable

The "difficult" poetry of Emily Dickinson and Paul Celan

> . . . you will come to it,
> the thing towards which you reason, the place where the flotsam
> of the meanings is put down
> and the shore
> holds.
>
> (Jorie Graham, "On Difficulty," 1995, p. 55)

Wilfred Bion (1965), toward the end of his career, wrote that his understanding of patients was "by virtue of an aesthetic rather than a scientific experience" (p. 52). It is in this spirit that we pursue the analogy between poetic and psychoanalytic understanding. Two questions underlie our inquiry: Can we get something out of poems we don't really "get," and can we successfully treat patients whose inner life remains hidden from our empathic inquiry? We will look at two poets, Emily Dickinson and Paul Celan, who use the elusivity of their verse to chronicle elusive – and traumatic – mental states. Let's plunge in.

Emily Dickinson

Emily Dickinson's poems (1960) are lucidly opaque. The sources of the opacity – her personal isolation, her isolation as a woman writer, the essentially hermetic nature of her vision – are endlessly debatable. But the fact that we come back again and again to poems that resist all efforts at paraphrase speaks to her unique genius. A single phrase, "My life had stood – a loaded gun" (poem 754, p. 369), or "Heavenly Hurt, it gives us" (Poem 258, p. 118), can turn and turn in our minds for a lifetime, never settling, always reaching beyond what we can know about a life. Or the poem we will examine here (1960, Poem 280, pp. 128–129), which begins, "I felt a Funeral, in my Brain." To read this poem is to step off a cliff. It begins,

> I felt a Funeral, in my Brain,
> And Mourners to and fro
> Kept treading – treading – till it seemed
> That Sense was breaking through –
>
> And when they all were seated,
> A Service, like a Drum –
> Kept beating – beating – till I thought
> My Mind was going numb –

Two contrary impulses hit the reader: a questioning one, "Why is the funeral in her brain, not in her mind?" and a sinking in, as to a place one already knew, a precognition, déjà vu. It is almost as if the straining for answers and the sinking are in competition: now "it seemed/That Sense was breaking through;" now the repetitive drumbeats that yield only numbness. Is the funeral in her brain because a part of her brain itself is dying/has died? the analyst/reader wants to ask the speaker. And the other kind of listening, a brain-to-brain, drumbeat-to-drumbeat knowing – beating, beating, the repetition of its awful insistence. And the equally awful rhyme: drum/numb. We notice that even as we read this poem on the page, its insistence shortens our breath.

One more comment on the funeral taking place in the brain: the mind is the organ of a subject. The brain is an object, a thing, capable of being dissected. The funeral could be for the speaker as subject, now mostly gone, save as a recorder of sensations, scrapings and beatings. The brain is an organ that can be apprehended proprioceptively, as opposed to the more abstract *mind*. The speaker is experiencing her own sensorium – including the workings of the brain that records it – mechanically, from the outside.

Recall from our first chapter George Atwood's patient saying "I am dead." The awful finality of the statement actually awakens us, tears at our heart. Similarly, our response to Dickinson's funeral is not to wear black and mourn. We are looking, longing to find the speaker. The declarative language of the poem arouses in us its opposite: impressionistic, implicit, nonverbal. We have some "sense" of the meaning "breaking through" – perhaps of someone imagining their own funeral – but it is tentative. To insist on a particular meaning, e.g., "the speaker is depressed" or "the speaker is having a kind of breakdown," is to be like the persons Keats (1959) famously condemns in his letter about *negative capability* as displaying "irritable reaching after fact and reason" (p. 261). Do we need our mind, like a trained dog, to fetch meanings? Are the drumbeats only the thump of her own malevolent thoughts? Or are they the thump of our own heartbeat, quickening as the poem casts a shade of dread?

Better to apprehend the poem as an aesthetic experience, the way Bion apprehends his patients. One key to this aesthetic experience is through an appreciation of form. Denise Levertov (1992), in her essay "Some Notes on Organic Form," refers to Gerard Manly Hopkins's invented word *inscape* "to denote intrinsic form, the pattern . . . of objects in a state of relation to each other" (p. 67). The objects in Dickinson's poem – mind, funeral, mourners, drum – create an inscape we apprehend aesthetically, as form, and that form in turn holds our emotional and intellectual responses.

One sense of the form here is of a bound space. The poem is in quatrains; four walls make a room. Lines two and four in each quatrain show a full rhyme. (We will see in a moment what happens when this pattern gets interrupted at the end with a slant rhyme.) And the capitals! The capitals punch us in the gut with the finality of their thingness.

Yet another sense of form implies a movement through space, a trajectory. Robert Hass, in his "A Little Book on Form" (2017), describes this view as the way the poem embodies "the energy of the gesture of its making" (p. 4). The gesture here seems to be of Dickinson's sinking into the associative details of her thought process: funeral to treading mourners to drumbeats to numbness. It foretells a sense of falling, which is dramatically borne out in the last stanza. A downward spiral. And for us as well, twisting and falling toward some painful realization.

The third stanza:

And then I heard them lift a Box
And creak across my Soul
With those same Boots of Lead, again,
Then Space – began to toll,

continues our inventory of the awful particulars. We are in a realm where the main sense is hearing. Treading, beating, creaking, tolling. Are we in the dark? We are certainly below the action. Is this a basement? Is the funeral on the floor above us? Who is in the coffin? Why are those leaden boots familiar? But these questions and the part of our mind that asks them are brushed aside by the force of associations.

The last line represents a turning. We harken, as to a new note in a depressed patient's speaking. The earlier dashes are gestures of rhythm, adding to the staccato. But here they make for a rest: "Then Space – began to toll." We've somehow arrived outside of our house/brain. And space, the universe, is agentic, is tolling. Though still funereal, this tolling seems different than the beating and the creaking and scraping of lead. And note the rhyme here: soul/toll. The speaker's suffering has been universalized. The last two stanzas bear this out:

> As all the Heavens were a Bell,
> And Being, but an Ear,
> And I, and Silence, some strange Race
> Wrecked, solitary, here –
>
> And then a Plank in Reason, broke,
> And I dropped down, and down –
> And hit a World, at every plunge,
> And Finished knowing – then.

A case could be made that the speaker of this poem is experiencing an alternation of states between suffering and consolation. The writing itself, the placing of experience into form, is consoling. Susan Howe (1985) has maintained that Emily Dickinson's true religion is poetry. The funereal tolling of space becomes something else – a cosmic dialogue between the Heavens and Being. Bell, being, race, here. The sounds are lengthening out a bit, in contrast to the still clipped wrecked, solitary, silence.

What is this cosmic chiming that Being harkens to? It is a suggestion of an order beyond the personal. But Dickinson is not going to settle for some pat religious consolation. The personal *I*, which a moment ago was surrounded by noise, returns. Here, though, it is associated with silence, as if outside the hearing that Being offers, the cosmic Bell. So we have three terms: Heaven, Being and *I*. William Blake (1970, p. 35) wrote that "Eternity is in love with the productions of time," but here is something else. Our *I*, our subjective self, has interrupted that love affair. The *I* is lost in silence.

It is a remarkable shift from the noise of the treading and beating of the first two stanzas. Is it a reverent silence? An alienation ("some strange race")? Both at once? It is wrecked and solitary. The word we circle back to is "numb" from line eight. Numb, not dead. The speaker is still present, still here. "Wrecked, solitary, here –" with its probe of a dash pointing us forward to the ultimate stanza. As a therapist, I find this word *here* and its dash enormously moving. What do a patient's silence and solitude say to us in our consulting room? If not "I'm here," God help us. In any case, this small moment of *here* provides a pause, a platform for the poem's final plunge.

The last stanza of Dickinson's poem sends me associatively, and perhaps protectively, to these lines from Denise Levertov's "The Goddess":

> She in whose lip service
> I passed my time,
> whose name I knew, but not her face,
> came upon me where I lay in Lie Castle!
>
> Flung me across the room, and
> room after room (hitting the wall, re-
> bounding – to the last
> sticky wall – wrenching away from it
> pulled hair out!
> (2013, pp. 112–113)

Levertov's poem describes a kind of initiation, not a breakdown. I am surely going to this poem to remind me that falling and bruising can be for our spiritual benefit, somewhere out beyond the planks of reason. Dickinson's last stanza again:

> And then a Plank in Reason, broke,
> And I dropped down, and down –
> And hit a World, at every plunge,
> And Finished knowing – then.

Down and down we plunge with the speaker, past plank after breaking plank of reason. If you hit a world at every plunge, you are bouncing between worlds, plural, through the awful and wonderful manifestations of creation. A mystical awakening? initiation? A death? Both? Certainly the violence of the dropping and the hitting are terrible. And the word *Finished* – the only verb in the poem that is capitalized. We are finished with knowing. Is this a knowing that must die to initiate Knowing? And here is the awful, amazing slant rhyme down/then. If we are finished with knowing, what then? Moses, despairing over the broken tablets, climbs Sinai again. God, sensing Moses's despair, offers him a consolation: "And I will take away mine hand, and thou shalt see my back parts: but my face shall not be seen" (Exodus 33:23). A knowing beyond seeing, the dark side of the moon.

Two other meanings of the ultimate line are possible, though they have different valences. The moment, *then*, might mark an irreversible descent into madness, a world of perpetual not knowing. Or "Finished knowing" might mark the end of an initiation, when the new knowledge has been completely imparted.

Both are true. The analyst and the reader must keep in mind the forward and the trailing edge of the transference (Tolpin, 2002). With a heart that breaks when our patients come to an awful pause in their story, marked by "then" and an implied dash, when we look together into the abyss where plank after plank of words and reason will fail us as we fall. But even as we plunge, a scrap of humor, of hope. A pun, as on the word "race," as the human race races to its destiny. Or in the last ringing rhyme of the penultimate stanza, valorizing our presence and our listening: "ear" and "here." A moment in a successful therapy when we could say together, "We are finished knowing, but perhaps we are not quite finished."

Paul Celan

Paul Celan was born in Romania. His parents were shot by the Nazis, but he escaped from a work camp. After the war, he landed in Paris, where he wrote poems in German. He drowned himself in the Seine in 1970. Such a summary trivializes the life, but it perhaps can function as an introduction to the poems, whose terseness evokes a world where narrative approaches, as a limit, the unsayable.

Katherine Washburn, one of Celan's translators, writes in her introduction to *Last Poems*, "Celan described the trajectory of his own poetic career as 'still geworden,' becoming silent" (1986, p. 10). But it is a silence that fills the white, blank space of the page. And hope, as if by inversion, lives in the interstices. If it lives anywhere at all. "Saint Celan/Pray for us," Denise Levertov writes in one of her last, posthumously published poems, "that we receive//at least a bruise/blue, blue, unfading,/we who accept survival" ("Thinking About Paul Celan," 2013, p. 1011).

Celan's relationship to the German language is particularly relevant to our time of mass exile and trauma, when many of our patients have experienced dislocation of one kind or another. Washburn writes,

> Like the traveler fluent in many languages, caught in a moment of great pain or emotional intensity, who breaks into his native language, this poet, whose final poems summon again and again the images of severed tongues, fingers lopped off from the (writing) hand, and mouths choked with earth or sealed against speech, required the slow richness and long deprivation of linguistic exile.
>
> (1986, p. ix)

Let's begin:

Dream-Driven

Dream-driven on the cir
cular track,
swollen,

two masks for one,
the dust of planets in hollowed
eyes.
          (1986, pp. 77–78)

(The poems are untitled in the manuscript. I have followed, for clarity. the translator's convention of using the first words as a title.)

"Mit Traumantrieb auf der Kreisbahn,/an/geschwelt," in the original. The dictionary definition of Kreisbahn is orbit, but this translation opts for indeterminacy. The literal offers us an entrance to the poem, which links the vagaries of dreaming to the inevitability of gravity, pulling a planet along its fixed orbit. In William Blake's gnostic-based symbolism, for example, the fixed orbits of the planets are a symbol of the time-bound fallen world, from which only the poetic imagination can free us. And here even our dreams, where the imagination holds sway, have been circumscribed. Each word is an isolated planet in space. Phrase by phrase, word by word they roll, punctuating the empty space. A presentation we who have treated the dissociated, the almost silent, may be familiar with.

"Dream-Driven" is from the posthumous collection *Force of Light*. The poems are titled only by an initial word or phrase. Words, lines, stanzas break off in mid-utterance. Here we can read slowly, as we cannot in our work with patients, pausing in the space each isolated phrase brings, as in the stanza break between the single word, "swollen," and "two masks for one," before we proceed. The bruised, isolated face in its circular orbit of fixed time requires two masks for one self, two personas. Private/public? Poet/person? Or, more likely, the day-to day-survivor and the self of infinite, inexpressible grief.

How can we "read" the white space, the silences? They are filled with two heartbeats, two breathings we can almost sense, ours and the speaker's. Two imaginations, tethered, despite decades of removal, by a co-incidence in time, to the same moment of discovery. Celan's poems force us back into our own imagination, his own selfhood, in an attempt to meet him in their silence. We have little else for them but our everything. In my childhood, the Holocaust was known only through silence, through sentences trailing off. My mother and aunt steamed the glue off stamps, erased the franking. Thrift that told of past deprivation. And the yelling that would break out. Were their faces too swollen from some collective memory of past trauma for the masks of daily life in sunny Los Angeles to fit? I seem, from the comfort of my Berkeley study, to have a quality of my own experience of dread with which to bind "swollen" and "masks."

Not to mention the "dust of planets" – a symbol of our utter unimportance. "Heavenly hurt it gives us," in Emily Dickinson's phrase, a sense that our pain is not to be leavened by God but ignored (or, God forbid, ordained). Such indifference grinds into our "hollowed [and here we pause pause pause for the beats needed before plunging into the photo-memory of the Shoah survivor's socket-bound] eyes." Celan in Paris, liberated from the war but twice benighted: by memory and by the cosmic indifference of clock-time.

Already in this quick and terrible poem, we need balm, respite, blindness. And the poet obliges:

> nightblind, dayblind,
> world blind,
>
> the poppy capsule within you
> goes down somewhere,
> silences
> a fellow star,
>
> the swimming domain of sorrow
> records another shadow,

I often fall back on neuroscience in my work with trauma victims. A hedge against my own overwhelm. An internet search on natural opioids yields, "Experiments in mice have shown that 'deleting' the natural opioid enkephalin, which is heavily expressed in the brain's amygdala, increases their fear, anxiety and aggressiveness. By contrast, increasing enkephalin or reducing its breakdown reduces these behaviors" (*Science Daily*, 2017). Comfort for me, at least, in thinking the brain contains its own mercy. Enough to let me reenter the poem, the liquid domain of another's sorrow, and the shadow it casts. My mind conjures a pied trout with its supple shadow on the glimmering mica streambed.

Reveries aside, the white space between the silenced star and the "swimming domain of sorrow" is worth pausing over, even if just to admit the paucity of our interpretive capacity. We do notice that, under the poppy's analgesic, space is populated with fellows, or at least fellow stars, fellow travelers in our time-bound orbits.

And now there is a change of register:

> it all does you good,
>
> the heartstone thrusts through its fan,
> no cooling
> at all,
>
> it all does you good,
> you sail, smolder and die down,

Who is this fey consoler who suddenly enters? The tip of the poet's irony trips up my attempt at emotional escape. I hate this new voice, hate all the times I've tried shallowly to allay the discomfort in my consulting room. I have no idea what "the heartstone thrusts through its fan" really means. I associate to a device, some engine intended for comfort, overheating. And the thought occurs, as the voice repeats, almost as a refrain, that "it all does you good" might be not some well-intended bourgeois but God himself, watching (or not watching) us sail forth, slowly burn up and return.

If Deus has absconded, what are we left with but a swarm, a plague of eyes, of earth itself:

> swarms of eyes pass the straits
> a blood clot enters the track,
> swarms of earth encourage you,
>
> all the weather in the universe
> is harvesting.

I have found that when we have completely lost a patient's thread, it is best not to comment, to hope that something will become clearer with time. Perhaps that applies here as well. Is it the translation? – after all, these poems seem nearly impossible to translate. Not here, I suspect. In my edition, the gap between "you sail, smolder and die down" and "swarms of eyes pass the straits" encompasses a page break. But something besides the typography breaks here. Beyond my one association to the Biblical swarms, I'm at a loss. Images atomize. Blood clots in the track, the orbit of our lives. I think, with blood clots, of a stroke. And perhaps this is where we are: in a kind of aphasia, where meaning and expression are severed. But in the German, Celan's mother's language, the swarm of eyes is countered by the coined word "Erdshchwarme," a swarm of earth-speech. Earth-comfort, "dir zu," to you, my heart, my intimate. And then, a stanza break, longer and blanker, it seems, then all the others. Time inside it to wonder, is the earthswarm nature, the waiting grave, or perhaps both?

The last couplet: "all the weather in the universe/is harvesting. Just as, in our clinical analogy fantasy, we are about to call time, the patient speaks. The German more clipped than the English translation: "das Wetter im All/ halt Ernte." Perhaps with better German. . . . The English looks like a sentence but isn't. Is that the point? Not even two masks, the mother's tongue or the recurring cycles of weather and harvest or stars in the universe, can cohere, can hold us together.

But the poem has led us so deep we do not despair. We are beneath the shells, the *klipot* in the Kaballah that Celan knew, the masks that hide our original radiance. The planets, the poppy, the shadows. If not to a higher order, then the poem pertains at least to its own, human order, a small victory over the tangle of memory.

I have deliberately chosen two poets to discuss here whose work sets out to describe all-but-indescribable mental states. Dickinson's poems, like some patients, require empathy and patience but eventually reward our trying. We feel that we are inside her world and that our world has grown larger through the encounter. Celan, whose pain is of a different order, brings us to a point of compassion beyond empathic understanding. We stand in the silences, in the fragments of language, and marvel and despair at the same time, as the author must have.

Case example

Celia was the mother of a school-age child when she first came to see me. At the time of this writing, her daughter has finished college, and Celia has launched herself in a career. What is notable about my work with Celia, and the reason I include it here, is that some part of her story, indeed of her psyche itself, remained opaque to me. Our long work together has taught me to let that opacity be, not to poke at it with my therapeutic insistence on fact and certainty. I say "taught me" as if it were a smooth learning curve. In fact, my interpretive pokings or diagnostic impressions almost always disrupted the transference, sometimes traumatically for both of us.

It took me many years to discover that the problem wasn't a failure of empathy or clinical understanding. The problem was with the endeavor itself. My insistence on framing her problem in any way – rather than just being present – was disruptive to her psychic order. Affect regulation problem? Attachment disruption? Early history of sexual abuse (of which there were plenty of hints)? Some other repressed trauma? The framing itself, the search for clinical knowing of any kind, beyond what Celia knew of herself, was destabilizing. Was this because we were getting close to something emotionally unbearable? Was it a deep-seated cultural resentment? (She always minimized my attempts to go there – "that's just your white good-guy complex talking.")

At times, especially early on, we would get into angry fights, fights in which I ended up feeling that I was fighting for my right to think for myself at all. At other times, when I could get over myself, our work functioned as a respite from the chaos of her outside life. Celia had a large family of three brothers and two sisters. She was the second oldest. Her family was originally from Puerto Rico but had been in the area for two generations. Celia spoke only halting Spanish. It was a working-class but comfortable family, with deep roots in a multiethnic part of Oakland. Her father worked in the county assessor's office. Her mother had also worked for the county, in the welfare office, but had had to quit, at the time Celia started therapy, because of her worsening multiple sclerosis. Her mother was a stern if overwhelmed woman who valued order above all else. A sensitive child prone to nightmares, Celia remembers being punished for waking up at night and was often the butt of family jokes. Her mother did little to intervene, but any critical-sounding comments about her mother on my part would lead Celia to stick up for her, emphasizing how hard she worked to make up for her disability and all the cultural opportunities she gave the children.

In her adult life, Celia had times when she would plunge herself into the family drama. She felt that one of her sisters in particular was out to get her. When she first started to see me, she was working as a playground supervisor at a parochial elementary school. When she lost that job, she was convinced that her sister Rita had planted lies with the parish priest. At times, Celia sounded delusional, as when she reported cars going by her house, shouting insulting things to her and calling her by name. At other times, Celia would break off from family and friendships, isolate herself and grieve bitterly that her family and friends so often betrayed her.

Like the poems in this chapter, work with Celia required a surrender of one kind of knowing in favor of another. And this other kind of knowing revealed a spiritual, aesthetic side of Celia that I came to treasure and love. She dressed flamboyantly, but with exquisite taste. A spiritual seeker, she moved in and out of various New Age persuasions, of which there were many in the Bay Area. She was very insightful about their weaknesses – "They're a bunch of bored white girls," "They would like to be Christians, but their friends would disapprove." All her criticisms came with a dose of love for her fellow seekers on the spiritual path. After these sojourns, she would come back to the Church and throw herself into the local parish activities. Her family, especially her mother, was often critical, but she just shrugged their judgments off. Throughout the vicissitudes of her spiritual life, which often tracked the vicissitudes of her mental state, Celia never failed to sacrifice for her daughter, to love and support her. Despite living in near poverty, she found a way to pay for her daughter's dream of attending UC Berkeley.

Celia had tremendous rage at men. She maintained that she would like to have been a lesbian but, beyond a few affairs, had not managed it. She had a long-term relationship with an Anglo man she met after her daughter was born, but she was constantly enraged at him for his neglect and forgetfulness. The relationship had ceased being romantic years ago. Celia had experimented sexually when she was young, but now the thought of being touched revolted her. All of this seemed consistent with a history of sexual abuse, and there were stories about being terrified as a child of a friend of her father's, but as if by mutual consent, we didn't go there. I thought her mother's coldness and lack of empathy for her nightmares went beyond the realm of normal, but efforts to go into that were met with resistance, anger or an announcement that she was perfectly fine and planned to quit therapy. What did seem to help were empathic interpretations that didn't look for depth or causation, on the order of "You are very sensitive to your siblings' envy. It's hard for you to succeed when they are struggling."

Over the course of our work, there were relatively uneventful periods when Celia made a lot of progress. She made new friends and worked her way through school, with a dual major in art and education. She eventually got a job as an art teacher in a public high school, and her textile art began to be shown and recognized. Her daughter, though nearby, moved onto campus and did not see her regularly. Celia's anger and grief at this loss seemed to me to be normal – that is considerable.

Recently, I hazarded an interpretation about her mother, which received a nod of "that's possible." Celia was saying that nothing in her childhood seemed to account for the depth of her problems. "My mother didn't hit me, she didn't hate me. The house was always orderly; we always had everything we needed. A couple of sharp looks, but mostly I remember her face as kind of blank. With six kids, who can blame her?" "Perhaps that blankness is a bigger deal then we think," I replied. "Research on mothers and babies has shown that a blank expression can be pretty disruptive to the baby's development." "It used to bother me so much that I couldn't really remember what might have happened to me as a child, that I might never really know," Celia stated with a touch of sadness. "Maybe there are more things like that than we like to think," I replied.

A narrative structure, the emergence of a coherent and mutually acknowledged understanding of her history or of our transference relationship, never developed. I came to see that Celia's parts were irreducible – her paranoia, her drama, her persistence, her flamboyance, her creativity. From the point of view that Bion (1965) espoused in our epigraph, she could only be appreciated aesthetically.

Poets of indeterminate or multiple meanings, like Dickinson, and poets like Celan, who express the otherwise inexpressible with enigma and silence, reward tenacity. This is true for patients like Celia as well, where hanging in there for a long time becomes the meaning of the work itself.

Part II

A note on Part II

In addition to commenting on the human condition, the poets we turn to now try to improve it. You can trace an arc between the nation-founding epic of Virgil, which describes how a hero can lead recovery from a great catastrophe, to the personal redemption myth of Dante to the romantic movement of Blake offering art and poetry as a path to liberation. And on through Whitman's great – and uniquely American – act of self-invention to Steven's celebrating the poet's imagination as the source of comfort in a world where God has failed us. The local American landscape itself is the hero in William Carlos Williams, celebrated in plain language through close observation, while Claudia Rankine documents the survival of black people in a world of overt and implicit racism.

Chapter 6

Meeting the father in the underworld
Virgil's *Aeneid*, Book VI

"In tears as he speaks, Aeneas loosens out sail/And gives the whole fleet its head" (Virgil, 2016, VI, 1–2, p. 3). So begins Book VI of Virgil's *Aeneid*. True to the hero's code, he turns his grief into freedom of motion. I can feel this move in myself, sense it in my patients. It is culturally gendered male but increasingly available to anyone. It is particularly American as well, moving out and moving on to escape our past. But despite this opening, Book VI describes a different journey, a different energy, downward and inward. Here is Aeneas' voyage into the underworld, the land of the dead, where he meets figures from his traumatic past and is promised an heroic future.

The *Aeneid*, along with its Grecocenteic counterpart the *Odyssey*, are postlapsarian. They depict not the founding of a civilization but its recovery. Both tell of the journey that follows the cataclysmic destruction of Troy, which leaves a legacy of trauma for both parties: for the victorious Greeks a journey home, for the vanquished Trojans a journey into exile. Both epics center around a series of trials that presage a reunion – for Odysseus, with Penelope; for Aeneas, with his dead father in the underworld. For the victor, the reward is an escape from history into domestic peace. For Aeneas, the vanquished, the ultimate reward is a redemptive entrance into history, with the triumphal founding of Rome.

Whether the hero is struggling to find his way home or struggling to found a new kingdom, the starting point of both epics resembles the moment in life when many patients enter therapy. Their lives have been disrupted by the violent upwelling of rivalries and jealousies of the kind that led to the Trojan War or threatened by the growing sense that something inside them is irredeemably broken. The heroes are literally and figuratively at sea.

This chapter tracks an iteration of one such catalyst, the death or loss of the father and the longing to refind him, as described in Book VI. Seamus Heaney's (Virgil, 2016) magnificent new translation offers us a version that emphasizes the hero's vulnerability. We will see how a reading of the mythic reunion of Aeneas and his father, Anchises, in the underworld might shed light on the experience of those patients (particularly men) who long for a closer relationship with their fathers as well as a renewed sense of their own vitality.

The poem suggests that this requires not a journey upward, toward glory, but a journey downward, into the unconscious. Freud (1981), equating the underworld with the unconscious, quotes on the title page of *The Interpretation of Dreams* Juno's famous curse from Book VII of the *Aeneid*, "If I cannot sway the heavens, I'll wake the power of hell." In keeping with my relational approach, I will be looking at the way Virgil's narrative tracks both intrapsychic conflicts and interpersonal longings and disappointments.

Aeneas loses his wife and comrades to the ravages of war but escapes from Troy with his son and his father on his back. He flees out to sea with a small band of men and, after many exploits and trials, including his father's death, lands in Italy. It has been foretold that he will found there the triumphant city-state of Rome; he will engage in a series of battles that end with his victory. Virgil's epic offers the restoration of the self through the hero's reclaiming his imperial power and invincibility. This is in stark contrast to tragic story of Oedipus that Freud found so central, where the action collapses inwardly, to a moment of terrible self-realization. Oedipus must now live, blinded with the knowledge of his transgression, just as Freud's patients must live with (and hopefully tame) the darker urges of their nature. Freud's tragic man versus Virgil's hero: the contrast bears on the question, what do we restore when restore a vital sense of selfhood? Is it the narcissistic fantasy of invincibility or a self whose aliveness derives from the intimate knowledge of loss and vulnerability?

Book VI catches Aeneas on the cusp of this question, still in his grief and willing to risk any peril for a chance to meet again his father. Here's poet Robert Duncan in his essay "The Truth and Life of Myth" (1968a), describing the way wrath and love overlap in the poetic imagination: "Reason falters, but our mythic, our deepest poetic sense, recognizes and greets as truth the proclamation that the Son brings, that just this Wrathful

Father is the First Person of Love. [The] son's cry to the father might be too the cry of the artist to the form he obeys" (p. 24).

The son's cry to the father underlies Aeneas's journey to the underworld, but the father does not transform into a figure of love. Instead, he remains a phantom, one who sets the son out on a series of battles, an agenda of revenge and unfinished business. As analysts, listening to the anguished cry of the son, we might prove more responsive than Anchises, Aeneas's father. We might hear the longing for touch as an undertone, the announcement of a new order, an order based in love not rage. Aeneas's comrades, his wife, his father are all left on the bloody ground of Troy. Are the wounds of war excised by his later triumphs? Or must there be a reckoning, a journey to find what is hidden underground, in particular his dead father. We will focus here on the complex relationship of the father and the son and on the posttraumatic search for a restorative father figure.

After the fall

In his groundbreaking reformulation of the Oedipus complex, Greenberg (1991) describes a vignette of a patient who, after a game of tennis with his father, notes that the father seemed weak and tired. The father, rather than being a threatening rival, becomes a source of deidealization and lost vitality. The task is not to neutralize or sublimate drives but to establish relationship. In the mythic backstory, Aeneas, conceived in the union of Anchises and Aphrodite, is raised by nymphs until age five (the age Freud identified as the critical period for oedipal development) and then returned to Anchises. Anchises has been admonished never to tell that he has lain with the Goddess but lapses into bragging about it and is punished by Zeus with lameness via a lightning bolt to the foot. He is thus a castrated rather than a castrating father. In an era when many of our patients suffer from father-longing rather than father-dominance, this motif rings especially true.

Because of his father's lameness, Aeneas must carry Anchises on his back through the ruins of Troy as well as lead his young son by the hand:

So come, dear father, climb up onto my shoulders!
I will carry you on my back. This labor of love
will never wear me down. Whatever befalls us now,
we both will share one peril, one path to safety.
(Virgil, 2006, II, 880–883, p. 99)

Aeneas thinks his wife, Creusa, is following, but when he discovers her missing, he goes back into the ruins, only to find her ghost, who reveals his fate and urges him to look after their son. Then, in a terrible passage that foreshadows his reunion with his father, he tries to embrace her, only to find "her phantom/sifting through my fingers,/light as wind, quick as a dream in flight" (II, 984–986, p. 102). The poem's narrative describes the challenges and misadventures Aeneas encounters after he leaves Troy, all the time trying to get to the shores of Italy. In a famously understated passage in Book III, Anchises dies:

> . . . Here, after all the blows
> of the sea and storm I lost my father, my mainstay
> in every danger and defeat . . .
> (Virgil, 2006, III, 818–820, p. 126)

Aeneas arrives at Cumae

Book VI opens with Aeneas still grief-stricken, crying as he makes landfall on Cumae, in Sicily, home of the oracle Sibyl he must consult. He and his shipmates pass the sacred grove of Diana, the hill where Dedalus ended his flight, and a fascinating urn carved in relief with mythological references. Then they arrive at the Sibyl's cave. After a gloomy prophecy that Aeneas seems almost to shrug off, he gets to his real concern – he implores the Sibyl for "One face to face meeting with my dear father." In this he resembles a patient who, ignoring red flags flying every which way, sticks to the one issue that is dominating his subjective world. He implores the prophetess to:

> Point out the road, open the holy doors wide.
> On these shoulders I bore him through flames
> And a thousand enemy spears. In the thick of the fighting
> I saved him, and he was at my side then
> On all my sea-crossings, battling tempests and tides,
> A man in old age, worn out, not meant for duress.
> He too it was who half-prayed, half-ordered me
> To make this approach, to find and petition you.
> Wherefore have pity, O most gracious one
> On a son and a father, for you have the power.
> (Virgil, 2016, VI, 153–163, p. 15)

In addition to the heartbreaking longing for a reunion after death, there is a slight undertone of obligation here, perhaps even of guilt. Aeneas's father was "worn out, not meant for duress" (wonderful word choice, duress! Implying not only stress but a hint of coercion). Anchises "half-prayed, half-ordered me" to seek a way to see him.

Exhausted from war and trials, called on to fight on and on in behalf of the collective, Aeneas tries to convince the Sybil to grant his boon. "Let me, a living person, enter the underworld, see my father, and return alive. I am at least as deserving as Orpheus," he argues, beginning a litany of those who have been granted visitation with the dead. In fact, he is more deserving than the others, he contends. "I am a descendent of Jove."

A drop of defensive grandiosity hiding the underlying vulnerability. Many of our patients in midlife are trying to sort out how much of their inner world is structured by *should*, represented here by the warrior's path, and how much is structured by loneliness and longing. The Sybil, as if she could discern Aeneas's vulnerability, warns him that it is the return to the land of the living that will prove arduous:

> It is easy to descend into Avernus.
> Death's dark door stands open day and night.
> But to retrace your steps and get back to upper air,
> That is the task that is the undertaking.
> (174–178, p. 15)

To me, a shot across our analytic bow. Far easier to cleverly unravel a self than to put one back together. Therapy is not a dig, a treasure hunt. The doors to the underworld – dreams, associations, transference – are always open. As are the doors of drugs, alcohol and sex, not to mention the spiritual doors of prayer and meditation. The return ticket is the one that will cost you. The building of psychic structure requires empathy, patience, relationship and a great deal of humility.

Or in the myth, the possession of the legendary golden bough – attained by some combination of luck and strength. A prepunched pass to transcendence:

> Hid in the thick of a tree is a golden bough
> Gold to the tip of its leaves and the base of its stem
> Sacred tradition declares to the queen of that place.
> (187–189, p. 17)

. . . No one is allowed
Down to Earth's hidden places unless he has first
Plucked this sprout of fledged god from its tree
And handed it over to fair Proserpina . . .

(191–194, p. 17)

By what technique or theory do we help our patients grab this magical
limb? Empathy, interpretation, relatedness, neuroscience? No, says the
Sibyl, it's ruled by fate:

. . . If fate has called you,
The bough will come away in your hand.
Otherwise, no strength you muster will break it,
Nor the hardest forged blade lop it off.

(200–203, p. 17)

Humbling stuff in our manualized age of "scientific" approaches to psychotherapy. But we can at least try to be present to moments when fate is
working and the work, as if by its own design, deepens.

Into the shadows

Aeneas wants to go big, but the Sybil says "not so fast." Braking as well as
prodding are part of the therapist's work. The initiation to the underworld
involves completing tasks in this one. The Sybil reminds him of some
unfinished business: he must give a proper burial to the one of his crew
who has died. That done, the door to the underworld, to the lost father, is
near at hand. Just as the funeral rites were concluding,

A pair of doves chanced down from the sky
In full view, and settled on the green grass;
In them the great hero knew his own mother's birds
And prayed and rejoiced: "O if a way can be found
Be you my guides . . .
And you, my goddess mother, do not abandon me
In this time of confusion."

(258–268, pp. 21–23)

A wish for a protective and guiding mother to enable him to find his father. And the dove/mothers do just that, "Now feeding, now flying ahead, at all times/Staying in view of the eyes that pursued them" (269–270, p. 23). Protecting him as he discovers "the fuming gorge, at Avernus," the door to the underworld. And right beside it, conveniently enough, his means of travel: "a tree that was two trees/In one, green leafed, yet reful-gent with gold" (273–274, p. 23).

The convenient location is a narrative trope, perhaps, eliding a long quest, but for our purposes a useful one. The door down is right at hand: a look, an emerging sense of self, a slight perturbation in the transference. And the enabling means is right at hand as well: two trees in one, ordinary and golden in equal measure. A lucky guess, a studied interpretation, a holding back, a bit of self-disclosure, a curious look, judicious silence. Out of our hands, really, a twist of analytic fate

The propitiating sacrifices made, Aeneas and Sibyl, his therapist/guide, go forth to discover "Mysteries and truths buried deep in the earth." There at the edge of the underworld, Aeneas must throw himself into the mouth of a cave, distract and escape horrible monsters and enter a world of lost and longing and suffering souls, all of them yearning for the unattainable light of day. What Aeneas finds in the underworld is a catalog of human suffering:

> . . . where pain
> And self-wounding thoughts have ensconced themselves.
> Here too are pallid diseases, the sorrows of age,
> Hunger that drives men to crime, agonies of the mind,
> Poverty that demeans . . .
>
> (364–368, pp. 29–31)

And this is just the outskirts. The journey here is a reversal of the psy-choanalytic that, if successful, traverses personal suffering to arrive at a place where the patient can bear it, especially in light of the realization that his suffering is human, not unique to him. Here the psyche is imme-diately assailed by the full range of human suffering. He is in hell. But we are reminded that in Goethe's great play, Faust asks Mephistopheles for a description of hell. "Why, this *is* hell," comes the reply, "nor are we out of it." "Self-wounding thoughts . . . pallid diseases, the sorrows of age/Hunger that drives men to crime, agonies of the mind,/Poverty that

demeans." . . . And, for toppers, "death-dealing war/And fanatical violence" (365–368, pp. 29–31). Here is the first of the Buddha's Four Noble
Truths: All life is suffering. In Heaney's version, informed perhaps by
memories of the recent Irish "troubles."

And then, at the gates themselves, "Lives without substance, phantoms,
apparitional forms":

> . . . two natured Centaurs
> And Scyllas, hundred headed Briareus, the Beast of Lerna
> Loathesome and hissing, and fire-fanged Chimaera;
> Gorgons and Harpies too, and the looming menace
> Of triple-fanged Geryon.
>
> (381–386, p. 31)

Every child knows the terror of the monstrous. For adults, a world
of nightmares, of psychosis. Perhaps what is symbolized here is the
terrible loss of the self, with all of its structures and attachments. A
workplace-crush exposed, a humiliating career reversal, the revelation
of a spouse's unfaithfulness. Or just the leaden ordinariness of one
more unbearable day. Such are the monstrosities that guard our gates
of hell.

Now Aeneas descends from the collective to the personal. The road
to the father lies through the relationship to the feminine. In order to
reunite with the father, Aeneas must first pass through a pair of tableaux
that depict two dreaded outcomes of the mother/son relationship: either
the son murders the mother/lover or the devouring mother murders him.

So the news I got was true: Dido and Aeneas

In his journey to meet his father, Aeneas relives a terrible incident in which
his personal desires and his god-driven fate collided: his love affair with
Dido. Passing through the Fields of Mourning, Aeneas meets those "Who
suffered hard and cruel decline/In the thrall of an unremitting love" (595–
596, p. 47) and sees star-crossed lovers, a mother stabbed by her own son
and Caeneus "who in her time had known/Life as a man, thought fate had
now restored/The figure of the woman she once was" (601–603, p. 47).
He seems moved by these tragic stories then a bit stunned to encounter

his own beloved Dido among them, "still nursing her raw wound." Dido, who killed herself following Aeneas's abrupt, god-ordered departure from Carthage. The story is this: Dido and Aeneas meet and fall in love when he and his men land in Carthage; when the gods order Aeneas to leave and complete his journey, Dido builds a funeral pyre that he can view from the sea and throws herself into it. But not before she curses Aeneas and his offspring.

The idea that the dead embark on a kind of karmic journey – encountering those they have harmed – has antecedents in many traditions, including the Buddhist and Egyptian as well as the Catholic tradition of Purgatory. But Aeneas, like our patients, is alive, seeking to reverse a thrall that has overcome him. When

> . . . The Trojan came close and made out
> Her dimly wavering form among the shadows,
> He was like one who sees or imagines he has seen
> A new moon rising up among the clouds
> On the first day of the month
>
> (606–610, p. 47)

Stunning simile: seen and unseen, the new moon, behind clouds. The referent is not, or not only, Dido, but Aeneas's own seeing. It is a flash of recognition, unformed, half-formed, fleshed out in the mind. A new moon, a new month, a glimpse of a new analytic possibility, perhaps just a glance, a look, an affect, something twice hidden, by clouds and shadow. Is it seen or just imagined?

In the mythic trope of the hero's journey, Dido is one more waylay, one more temptation. But something more than just a test passed, a triumph of piety and obedience over the heart, is implied in Aeneas's underworld encounter:

> He wept and spoke these loving, tender words
> "Unhappy Dido! So the news I got was true,
> That you had left the world, had taken a sword
> And bade your laws farewell. Was I, O was I to blame
> For your death?"
>
> (611–614, pp. 47–48)

But this moment of self-doubt is immediately replaced by justification:

> . . . I swear by the stars, by the powers
> Above and any truth there may be under the earth,
> I embarked from your shore, my queen, unwillingly.
> Orders from the gods, which compel me now
> To travel among shades in this mouldering world.
>   (615–620, p. 49)

Dido is unconvinced, refusing to meet Aeneas's eyes or acknowledge his existence. 'How could I believe," he asks to no one in particular, "My going would devastate you with such grief?" (VI, 621–622, p. 49). Is there a bit of false naivete here? If so, then his next question is pure projection: "Is there something you are trying to avoid?" But then, at last, a breakthrough of his suppressed affect, as the finality of his loss hits him: "These words I'm saying to you are the last/Fate will permit me, ever" and then "Tears welling up inside him." Virgil describes Dido as having a "fierce gaze," but to my ear she seems more traumatized, frozen or dissociated than fierce as she "showed no sign. . ." of having heard, no more//Than if her features had been carved in flint/Or Parian marble" (VI, 624–635, p. 49).

The scene ends with a tableau of almost unendurable poignancy, as Aeneas watches his beloved Dido returned to the comforting arms of Sychaeus, her former husband, who "feels for her pain/And reciprocates the love she bears him still" (637–638, p. 49). The man of action is usurped by the man of empathy and forgiveness. In the end, Aeneas is left alone with his unresolved grief:

> While Aeneas, no less stricken by the injustice
> Of her fate, gazes into the distance after her,
> Gazes through tears, and pities her as she goes.
>   (639–641, pp. 49–50)

Love bites: the encounter with Deiphobus

As if the author were eager to get back to the world of heroes and actions, the poem now jump-cuts to a field of "Those renowned in war." After a catalog of Trojan heroes and a somewhat gratuitous slap at the Greeks, who cower and flee when they see Aeneas in his armor, the poet gets back to his current subject – the trouble between men and women and the perfidy of the latter. Aeneas meets a hero "mutilated in every part," Deiphobus, son of Priam,

> . . . his face
> In shreds – his face and his two hands –
> Ears torn from his head, and his nostrils
> (A low dishonorable wounding, this)
> His nostrils cut away.
> (666–669, p. 53)

The mind races to our latest terrorism victims or to the seats on the Paris Metro still in the 60s reserved for the *mutiles de guerre*, and Aeneas assumes the same:

> . . . The story I heard was this:
> On the last night in Troy, you waded in Greek blood
> Till you fell exhausted, fell like a dead man
> On a heap of their slobbered corpses . . .
> (676–679, p. 53)

but it turns out that Deiphobus's wounds were administered by the perfidious Helen, a literal *femme fatale*. He is a *mutilé d'amour*:

> . . . What you see
> Are the love bites she left me in remembrance
> Of that last night.
> (691–694, p. 53)

The final revenge of a woman handed around like a prize horse.

Virtuous, victimized Dido; violated, violent Helen. Two female archetypes, and in Aeneas and Deiphobus, two heroes, one guilty, one shredded. The lopped-off ears and nose leading the mind to wander and wonder over the rest of his anatomy. The road to the father, it seems, runs through a graphic encounter with the feminine. And a reckoning of our misuse of her. Aeneas, the seducer, whom the gods summon from the marriage bed into history. His shade perhaps falls on our contemporary absentee husbands. And Deiphobus, the warrior rapist, who is "given" Helen as a prize after his brother's demise. For which she invokes her horrible revenge, signaling the Greek soldiers in the horse, then mutilating her captor/husband. Is this comrade in arms also a comrade in shadows meant to indicate a part of Aeneas he must reckon with before he can meet his father?

"Gods!" implores Deiphobus after retelling his trauma, "Retaliate! Strike the Greeks with all due punishment." But then, as if coming to his senses, fury subsides, replaced by curiosity: "But you," he says to Aeneas, "What about you?" The living and dead, their emotions curbed, meet as equals, as in a session that appears to be an uneventful telling of the week but in fact indicates a shift in the transference from disruption to function. The patient, in effect, coming up for air, noticing that the analyst is still there.

A dream with wings: Aeneas meets his father

After the Sibyl describes Tartarus, with its vast halls of torture, she leads Aeneas up to Elysium. First, as if to mark the transition from a world of woe to one of valor, he plants the golden bough at the gate, not failing to list poets among the virtuous "with headbands white as snow/tied around their brows" (VI, 899–900, p. 69). Here we find Orpheus tuning his lyre, the seed-stock of the Trojan heroes, wounded warriors, priests of Apollo, and those "Whose discoveries improved our arts or ease, and those/Remembered for a lifetime of serving others" (VI, 896–897, p. 69).

It's a kind of pastoral summer camp. When they ask where to find Anchises, Museus, poet-spokesman for the "Happy Spirits," replies,

> None of us has one definite home place.
> We haunt the shadowy woods, bed down on riverbanks,
> On meadowland in earshot of running streams.
> (909–911, p. 69)

But eventually Anchises is discovered "Off in a deep valley/Surveying and reviewing the souls consigned there" (VI, 917–918, p. 71), preparing virtuous Trojan souls for reincarnation and their mission to found and populate Rome.

But this pastoral set piece with its undertone of imperial drum rolls is pierced through the heart by the emotional climax of Book VI: Aeneas's meeting with his father. Not as he perhaps unconsciously hoped for, in the flesh, but as a bodiless spirit. A close reading of this passage reveals it is

more joyous and fulfilling for the dead father than the living son. When he
sees Aeneas, Anchises raises his arms and cries out,

> . . . At last! Are you here at last?
> I have always trusted that your sense of right
> Would prevail and keep you going to the end.
> And am I now allowed to see your face,
> My son, and hear you talk, and talk to you myself?
>
> (926–929, p. 71)

To see, to be seen, to talk, enough for the spirit father, but the son longs
to touch as well. For the son, a disappointing reenactment of the visions
that had led him on through his journey:

> Often and often, father, you would appear to me,
> Your sad shade would appear, and that kept me going
> To this end. My ships are anchored in the Tuscan sea.
> Let me take your hand, my father, O let me, and do not
> Hold back from my embrace. And as he spoke, he wept.
>
> (637–641, pp. 71–72)

This passage of incredible subtlety reveals the imbalance of longing and
need between father and son. The son has lived in service to the lame
father, carrying him out of Troy and onto his ship. The elusive representation of his father has driven him on through danger, through his finding the
golden bough and through the terrifying and piteous journey underground.
Stories and sight are enough for the father, who can live again vicariously
through his son's exploits. The son, though, wants the consoling truth of
physical contact, even as he fears that his father will hold back or recoil.
It would seem the tragedy here is not just mediated by death, but by some
residue of their living relationship. *May their memory be as a blessing*, the
rabbi intones after chanting the Kaddish, the Jewish memorial prayer. But
here is no consolation. The inviolate physical boundary between the living
and the dead is sorrowfully enacted:

> Three times he tried to reach arms around neck.
> Three times the form, reached for in vain, escaped
> Like a breeze between his hands, a dream on wings.
>
> (942–944, p. 72)

Even the magical number three, as in wishes, will not suffice to quench the son's longing for a father's lost embrace. For this hero, who has undergone trial after trial, the dead remain dead. And his grief remains, in the moment when he embraces air, inconsolable.

Dénouement: the denial of grief

The pathos of Aeneas's arms passing through his father's insubstantial form is not the end of Book VI. After a brief metaphysical digression, Anchises leads his son to a view of the souls of fallen Trojan soldiers, ready to cross the river Lethe and be reborn as Roman Legions, destined to imperial glory. Seamus Heaney himself, in an unfinished afterword to the translation appended to the published work, criticizes this ending:

> For the contemporary reader, [Book VI] is the best of books and the worst of books. . . . Best because of its mythopoeic visions, the twilight fetch of its language, the pathos of the many encounters it allows the living Aeneas with his familiar dead. Worst because of its imperial certitude, its celebration of Rome's manifest destiny, and the catalog of Roman heroes.
>
> (Heaney, 2016, p. 95)

The best and worst aspects of the Book VI text that Heaney refers to can be seen as psychologically related. Unable to offer Aeneas the longed-for physical touch, Anchises offers him two consolations for his personal loss and for the traumatic events at Troy: a brief metaphysical exposition of reincarnation and the passages Heaney alludes to in which the glorious and gory history of the Roman Empire is temporally inverted and recast as prophecy.

A contemporary explanation of the connection between grief and militarism comes from Robert Stolorow. It is possible to read Anchises's prediction of imperial triumph as a defense against what Stolorow (2007) has described as the embeddedness of everyday life in finitude. Such embeddedness, Stolorow (2012) continues, is often denied through "forms of discourse that serve to cover over our human finiteness and the finiteness of all those we love. We succumb to a kind of forgetfulness of our finite kind of being."

> Such forgetfulness began soon after 9/11, as Americans fell prey to the rhetoric of the Bush administration, which declared war on global terrorism and drew America into a grandiose, holy crusade that enabled

Americans to feel delivered from trauma, chosen by God to rid the world of evil and to bring their way of life (= goodness) to every people on earth. Through such resurrective ideology and its rhetoric of evil, Americans could evade the excruciating existential vulnerability that had been exposed by the attack and once again feel great, powerful, and godlike (paragraph 3).

Stolorow's term "resurrective ideology" is particularly useful for our discussion, linking as it does Book VI's catalog of Rome's triumph and the description of the soul's passage from trauma to resurrection.

Psychologically, these resurrective ideologies amount to a denial or suppression of Aeneas's grief: his comrades murdered and disfigured by a senseless war brought on by hubris and lust, his beloved Dido driven to suicide by his obedience to the gods, his longed-for reunion with his father physically unconsummated. Denial of grief and vulnerability requires a denigration of the body, since that is where we feel. Anchises tells his son, "It is from the body/that fear and desire, grief and delight derive." The body, he continues, is where "we live in the darkness of its prison house" (VI, 990–992, p. 75). From this prison house, after eons of purging their sins, souls will be reborn in a new body of soldiers and emperors, who are destined "to make our name illustrious."

The project that Freud invented was to help his patients bear this kind of grief, without resort to metaphysics or violence-infused grandiosity. For the more ancient Homer, the second of his two great heroic epics with a restoration of love and domestic happiness as Odysseus returns home to Ithaca. Perhaps it is not only grief and trauma, but the humiliation of defeat that denies this kind of consolation to Aeneas and his fellow Trojans. We can view the kind of sci-fi set piece that ends Book VI, with Trojan soldiers coming back to life and joining the triumphant legions, as a kind of defensive grandiosity, denying that we live in the body's prison house. What Anchises cannot offer Aeneas is exactly what our patients want from us: a holding, a home in their darkness, a place to renounce a lifetime of ruses.

Case example

Martin's father was a beloved figure in their hometown. The soccer coach of the high school, he also volunteered with local soccer clubs and was especially active in working with minority communities. This made it all the more confusing when Martin was exposed to his father's other side – inflicting mental and physical abuse in the name of toughening him up or teaching him how the world really works. He would make him practice his soccer skills in brutally hot weather without a break, one time resulting in a serious case of heat stroke. He would drop him, at age six, in dangerous parts of town, relying on his "survival skills" to find his way home. Complicating this picture was his mother's instability. A chronic alcoholic, she was often absent either physically or mentally. So Martin's father also took on much of the mothering. Which only made his outward idealizablity and inward cruelty harder for Martin to decode.

Martin lived a bifurcated adult life that seemed to have replicated his father's duality. He was married and had two children and a successful career. But he also frequented the dangerous and exciting world of the gay pickup scene. His preference was for extremely well-built, somewhat brutal men who would put him in humiliating and degrading situations.

In treatment, Martin's attitude toward his father alternated between loathing and admiration. He was very angry about how his father treated his mother and his sister (to whom he was especially cruel), and he justified his mother's drinking as a natural result of her marriage. But he also was drawn to some of his father's political and philosophical ideas about manhood and tried to live up to those expectations. It was a very complicated picture of identifications and disidentifications.

What took a long time to surface was Martin's sense of his father as a lonely, misunderstood man. Far from a hero or an oppressor, a view emerged of the father as a man in a loveless marriage who tried to give his son the best of his love. This of course didn't jibe with his earlier picture of a brutal bully, but Martin did not seem to notice or was untroubled by the contradiction. Martin now felt that his maintaining the charade of being a straight, upstanding family man was the least he could do to protect his father from disappointment.

For a long time, Martin's ambivalence toward his father did not show up in the transference. He was relieved that I accepted his dual life without judgments. He often defended his father, so I backed off from condemning his father's abuse. For the longest time, it seemed that his unmet longings for an accepting father, as well as for an empathic mother, were being met in treatment.

What didn't change was his avid participation in the gay demimonde. My alarm at his subjecting himself to the risk of AIDS (which was still going strong back then) kept growing. Perhaps emboldened by Heinz

Kohut's (1984) famous comment to a young patient who was driving reck-lessly, "You are a complete idiot" (p. 74), I decided I must confront this dangerous behavior. I told him in a strong voice that he had to take steps to start having safe sex, that he was putting himself, his family and all the progress we had made at risk.

I expected him to resist or have a hard time with this. What I didn't expect was his almost complete emotional collapse and withdrawal from treatment. However well intentioned, I had come to incarnate his father for him, shaming and humiliating him in the name of teaching him a lesson. What was worse, any attempt I made to inquire about what was going on, as well as any attempt to repair the disruption, seemed to fall on deaf ears. After weeks of mostly silence, I told him that I knew my confrontation had backfired, and I thought I understood why, but I didn't know how to repair it. To my surprise, this seemed to be a relief to Martin. "You want me to live for your sake," he told me. "You never asked whether I want to live or not."

Martin never did resolve his double life or settle on a unified view of his father during the treatment. But he did come out to his wife, who seemed to accept him, saying that she had suspected as much for some time.

It is not completely clear to me why I associated to Martin's case so strongly as I was completing this chapter. Martin, like Aeneas, is essen-tially motherless. Both were willing to endure almost any risk to connect with a strong father figure. Perhaps at some level, I found Martin's dual life, bifurcated between a heroic ideal and a more instinct-driven actuality, reminiscent of Aeneas – a life marked by a schism between daylight and the underworld.

But most profoundly there is the unsolvable longing for a loving father, a longing concretized in the moment Aeneas's hands pass through his father's shade and by Martin's collapse following my confrontation. There are many men who carry the added burden of their fathers' unfinished business. Trying to live it out becomes a substitute for having a real con-nection. Was it Anchises's agenda to have Aeneas found a great empire? And was it mine to have Martin give up his enlivening though life-threat-ening activity?

If Virgil the poet denies Aeneas the consoling reunion with a father in the underworld, he (Virgil) will get a chance to make up for it more than a millennium later. We turn now to Dante's *Divine Comedy*, in which Virgil acts as Dante's guide, his wise and consoling father figure on another epic journey through the lands of the dead.

Chapter 7

"I was sent here to save him"

Dante's *Purgatorio* as
therapeutic journey

I first read the *Commedia* in the early 70s. Out of college and out of ideas as to what to do with my life, I accepted a friend's invitation to caretake a 40-acre piece of property – second-growth redwoods and live oak – he had just purchased on a ridge overlooking the Pacific in northern Sonoma County. It turned out to be the second-wettest winter of the 20th century, and the only reliably dry place in the cabin was under the kitchen table, where I often found myself curled in my sleeping bag, reading John Ciardi's (Dante, 1961) translation of the *Divine Comedy*. I had hoped to further my literary education, but Ciardi's somewhat overwrought English and the dark view of human nature (and the darker penitence-tortures Dante describes) ended up hastening my self-deterioration. So each Wednesday, I would take the 90-minute drive to Marin County, descend the rain-slick Seaview Grade, cut inland at Jenner and follow the Russian River to 101, to show up at a therapist's office by 11:00.

One day, in an ironic rhyme with the *Commedia*'s famous opening, "Midway through my life I found/myself in a dark wood" (Dante, 2002, I:1–2, p. 3), I was literally lost in a dark second-growth forest. I had brought a notebook down to the Gualala River, but the visibility dropped to the point that I had trouble seeing my hand in front of my face. Boy Scout-trained, I made a bed and coverlet of cross-hatched redwood boughs and survived a wet but nonlethal night. I told my therapist the story the following week, shaken but also a bit proud.

I hadn't set out to pair Dante to therapy, but the match was a natural and has stayed with me ever since. With the publication of W.S. Merwin's (Dante, 2002) lucid and literary translation of the *Purgatorio*, I have had a chance to revisit that pairing. Merwin's translation, while faithful to the mythology, numerology and theology that underlie Dante's great vision, brings to the fore Dante's tender relationships – with Virgil and other fellow poets – that form the core of the narrative. This emphasis on the human, on the secular, marks the Purgatorio as the most psychological of the three *Cantica*. Merwin himself makes this point in his foreword: "In the language of modern psychology, the *Inferno* portrays the locked, unalterable ego, form after form of it, the self and its despair inseparable" (p. viii).

By contrast, the *Purgatorio* marks a moment of rebirth, of the start of a journey, not downward through despair but upward, toward love and healing. As Merwin points out, one of the first things that Dante and Virgil behold when they emerge from the tunnel that connects Hell to Purgatory is the planet Venus, "The beautiful planet that to love inclines us" (I:19, p. 3). Our ability to stand again on earth, to look up and see stars in the sky, marks a profound shift in any journey from despair to recovery. By mid-spring, I had left the existential solitude of Seaview Road, moved back to Berkeley and switched to a local (and more compatible) therapist, with whom I was to complete an almost 10-year treatment. Toward the end of Canto I, Dante gives this description, so powerfully reminiscent of my time on the Sonoma Coast:

> The Dawn was overcoming the pallor of daybreak
> which fled before it, so that I could see
> off in the distance, the trembling of the sea.
> $\qquad\qquad\qquad$ (I:115–117, p. 9)

Overview

Whereas Book VI of the Aeneid describes a descent toward a reunion with a lost father, the *Purgatorio* describes an ascent toward a reunion with the beloved. In a narrative of shape-shifting reminiscent of the shifting of analytic transferences, Beatrice, the beloved, is both the guide and the goal. She arranges the journey, takes over the instruction from Virgil at the entryway to the Earthly Paradise and then appears dressed in white on a throne on the Divine Imperium in the *Paradiso*. Given that contemporary psychoanalysis holds that wholeness and relatedness go hand in hand, the fact that Dante's great epic is both a journey to heal the self and a journey to love mark it as uniquely fit to guide that process.

What's more, a story in which the author, apparently suffering from mid-life depression, undertakes a healing journey with a close guide/ companion opens the text to our purpose. The entire journey is taken through a spirit world of hell, purgatory and paradise, which can be plausibly viewed as a map of our unconscious and conscious mind. Yet the aptness of this analogy bids us caution, for Dante's late-medieval epic is an allegory not just of personal rebirth but of spiritual and artistic rebirth as well.

"I was sent to him to save him," Virgil tells the inquiring Cato in Canto I of Dante's *Purgatorio*, "and there was no other way/than this one, on which I begin my journey" (I:61–63, p. 5). The moment marks a profound turning in the *Commedia* narrative from the underworld of hell to this world, this earth, where they stand at the base of a winding-trailed mountain. "His goal is liberty" (I:71, p. 6).

Before we begin, let me offer the briefest of summaries. Though it ostensibly takes place in the year 1300, the *Divine Comedy* was in fact written between 1308 and 1320, allowing much recasting of events that had already happened into prophecy. At the time of its writing, Dante was in exile from his native Florence due to political intrigue. Beatrice, whom Dante first glanced on when both were nine years old, is the object of his *amor*, or courtly love. Now, from her perch in heaven, she sees his lostness and spiritual desolation and decides to intervene. She summons the Latin poet Virgil, author of the *Aeneid*, the founding myth of Rome, to guide Dante's journey through the three realms of the dead. First they travel through the unredeemed world of the Inferno, which is beneath the earth in a hole dug out of the earth by Satan's fall from heaven. On Easter Sunday, 1300, Dante and Virgil emerge from a tunnel back onto the earth, at the outskirts of purgatory, which is a mountain extruded on the other side of the earth from Satan's fall. As they climb up the mountain, Dante and Virgil cross nine levels, representing the seven deadly sins plus two that represent those in Purgatory for circumstantial reasons, such as babies who died too young to confess or victims of violence who had no time to repent. Finally, they arrive at the summit, the Earthly Paradise or Garden of Eden. At this point, Virgil, who died a pagan and thus cannot enter heaven, disappears, and Beatrice takes over as Dante's guide up to Paradise.

Disruption and repair

The idea that our normal everyday functioning needs to be disrupted and then repaired in order for us to grow has many antecedents. In Greek drama, the *catastrophe* marked the moment of unraveling. A moment without repair in the tragedies, but with a sorting out or reconstruction of order in the comedies. The *Commedia* is a comedy because things do get sorted out, and Dante gets to glimpse Paradise. The entire *Commedia* can be seen as an imaginative attempt to repair Dante's state of despair over his exile and the death of his beloved Beatrice.

In infant development, patterns of disruption and repair have particular salience in the acquisition of a resilient and stable sense of self (Beebe and Lachmann, 2002). Beebe and Lachmann focus not on large or traumatic disruptions but the nontraumatic, moment-to-moment instances of mother and caregiver being out of sync with each other. The dyad's return to healthy functioning becomes an implicitly laid-down template for handling later disruptions. Kohut (1984) called these nontraumatic disruptions "optimal frustrations." In adult treatment, Beebe and Lachmann have stressed the importance of the therapist's naming and repairing transference disruptions in the overall curative process.

The entire structure of the *Purgatorio* can be viewed as a pattern of disruptions and repairs. It is only upon entering Purgatory that the repair of the soul becomes possible. As Archibald T. MacAllister writes, "The *Inferno* is all darkness and the *Paradiso* is all light, the *Purgatorio* is a mixture of the two" (1961, p. xiii). We are on earth, with its alteration of day and night, for one. The disruptions are created through the confrontation with the vices and their punishments; the repair is affected by the constant selfobject-restoring presence of Virgil, angels and other poets.

For example, in Canto XVI, on the periphery of the ledge of wrath, Dante encounters smoke so toxic that "it would not let my eyes stay open," so Virgil offers him his shoulder "as a blind man goes along behind his guide" (XVI:7, XVI:14, p. 153); Marco, one of the penitents, tells the pair, "if the smoke keeps us from seeing/each other, hearing will hold us together instead" (XVI:35–36, p. 155). A soothing voice affects the repair. "*Guarda che da me tu non sia mozzo,*" Virgil tells Dante: "Be careful not to be cut off from me" (XVI:15, p. 153). Yet inevitably he is cut off, both from Virgil and from his self, until a glimpse of light, a hint of a song of praise from a chorus of penitents, or a touch of his master's hand refinds him.

An allegory of self

The very fact that at a moment in my youth in the 20th century, I could find (or lose) myself in Dante's *Divine Comedy* from the 14th points to his singular achievement. Dante turned the particulars of his own life – beginning with a midlife depression in which "Death scarce could be more bitter" (2002, Inferno, I:7, p. 3) – into a work of art that both immortalizes and transcends those particulars. From the perspective of more than 40 years, I can see that I was drawn to the fact that Dante depicts an act of radical self-invention. He anticipates by 500 years the words of another radical poet, William Blake: "I must create a system, or be enslaved by another man's" (1970, pp. 151–152). Washed up on the beach by the receding tide of the 60s, self-invention was exactly what I was in need of.

The *Divine Comedy* is a unique hybrid, part epic, part allegory, part personal narrative. Dante turns his life, both the outer – his lifelong exile from Florence and the political chaos that caused it – and the inner – his deepest longings and despairs – into an allegory, an instructional tale of fall and redemption. Dante the poet turns Dante the character into both a pilgrim-everyman and a mythic hero. As the former, he is humble and vulnerable, often turning to his guide Virgil in perplexity and despair. As the latter, he slyly exposes many of his personal enemies and the despots of his time to condemnation and punishment while describing his own hardships and triumphs. He universalizes the particular and particularizes the universal.

The *Purgatorio* invokes three of the most important aspects of contemporary psychoanalysis: the shape-shifting of the transference, the meaning-making that emerges from the telling of a personal narrative in relationship to a responsive other and the overall arc of healing and redemption. Although it honors the form of a religious narrative, the *Commedia* is hardly limited by doctrine. (Indeed, some scholars believe that the Church had to find a way to incorporate rather than condemn it because of the enormity of Dante's achievement.) Dante's freedom to pick and choose between pagan, Christian and imaginative sources makes his work an apt source of analogies to the "secular religion" of psychoanalysis. He has placed a human figure from his own history, Beatrice, in the role that Mary usually plays in Christian allegory. In an ostensibly Christian poem, Christ barely appears, while a pagan poet, Virgil, leads him to salvation.

Virgil

In an act of exquisite tenderness, Virgil begins the "pilgrimage" by wetting his hands on the dew-covered dawn grass, then wiping the traces of tears off Dante's face, restoring "all that color of mine which Hell had hidden" (I:129, p. 9). A maternal gesture, echoed with exquisite pathos toward the end in Canto XXX when Dante turns to Virgil "with the confidence that a little child shows, running to its mother" (XXX:43–44, p. 295) only to find that "Virgil had left us" (XXX:49, p. 295). Then no power on earth could "prevent/my *dew-washed cheeks* from running dark with tears" (XXX:54, p. 295, emphasis added). A tender mother at the beginning of the journey and an absent, longed-for mother at the end. And in between, an all-knowing father, guiding, cajoling, explaining the landscape and introducing its inhabitants to Dante along their path.

Heinz Kohut's concept of the selfobject is useful in understanding the relationship of Virgil and Dante, as well as Dante's relationship to Beatrice and to his fellow poets. The key to this concept is that the object becomes an inextricable part of the self, experienced as simultaneously external and internal (Kohut, 1971, 1977, 1984). Based on the transferences his patients yearned to establish in treatment, Kohut identified the mirroring and idealizable selfobject transferences. In the first, the analyst tracks and reflects the patient's experience; in the second, he understands, soothes and transforms (Bollas, 1987) that experience. Kohut later added a third selfobject transference, in which the analyst is experienced as a twin or kindred spirit, alike in some profound way. As I have pointed out (Shaddock, 1998), these transferences have at some symbolic level a family analogy, with the mirroring of a mother, the idealizability of the father and the commonality of the siblings. Virgil, at various times in the narrative, fulfills all three of these transferences for Dante: a guiding father and a comforting mother, but also a fellow poet, a similar, a twin.

One therapist-like function that Virgil performs is interpreter of dreams. In Canto IX, just outside the gates of Purgatory, Dante has a dream in which an eagle swoops down with outspread wings and carries him up into a fire, where "it seemed it burned and I burned with it/and such was the heat of the imagined blaze/that my sleep could not but be broken by it" (IX:31–33, p. 85). Finding there is "no one beside me except my comfort," Dante turns to Virgil for explanation. "Do not be afraid," Virgil tells him. "Take heart, it is good to be where we are./Do not hold back, but unleash all your valor" (IX:46–47, p. 85). Apparently using a theory that sees dreams as reflecting outside reality, Virgil explains that while Dante was sleeping, "A lady came and said, 'I am Lucy./Let me take up this one who is asleep/and in that way ease him on his journey'" (IX:55–57, p. 85). The lady is Lucia, the spirit of light, who has borne him up to the very gate of Purgatory. Virgil makes mention of the fire, which foreshadows the wall of flame that Dante must pass through in Canto XXVII.

As in the *Aeneid*, the father/son relationship enacted by Virgil and Dante takes precedence over the mother/son. But here the relationship, rather than ending in profound disappointment and a resurrective warrior fantasy, prepares the son for his meeting with the divine female.

Beatrice

Writing in *La Vita Nuova* (1969), a book that is, among other things, a prose narrative of his devotion to Beatrice, Dante describes their tie as a source of both delight and obligation. At his first glimpse of her, "dressed in . . . a decorous and noble crimson, tied with a girdle and trimmed in a manner suited to her tender age," a voice sounds in his head, "Now your source of joy has been revealed." And a moment later, "Woe is me! for I shall often be impeded from now on" (pp. 29–30). Dante is here following the example of the Troubadour poets, for whom courtly love of an unavailable lady is the highest and most civilizing of emotions.

The spell, or, we might say, transference, which Dante falls into with Beatrice is built upon her desirability and her remoteness. When, nine years after he first glimpses her, now "dressed in purist white," she greets him out loud, he experiences "the height of bliss. . . . As this was the first time she had ever spoken to me, I was filled with such joy that, my senses reeling, I had to withdraw from the sight of others" (p. 31). Her perfect idealizability is preserved by her chaste unavailability. If this is an erotic transference, it is built on the most abstinent of treatments imaginable.

Ten years after her death, it is Beatrice, concerned about the state of Dante's soul, who arranges Dante's redemptive journey, recruiting Virgil as his guide and securing the necessary permissions for a living person to pass through the land of the dead. A kind of divine intervention.

Dante's worshipful devotion to an unattainable female marks an historic turn toward the divine feminine, the source of refinement, inspiration, and ultimately, salvation. Petrarch, Dante's younger contemporary, wrote,

> What little I know of love is her gift
> My glimpse of perfect grace, and my ability
> To follow it are hers; my knowledge
> That want men want mostly is worthless.
>   (1981, p. 11)

In a similar vein, Virgil asks Dante in Canto VI to defer some of his questions until he meets with Beatrice at the top of the mountain; she, in Ciardi's translation, "will become your lamp/between the truth and mere intelligence" (1961, p. 75). Whether derived from years of therapeutic slogging through the quotidian details of a life or from an intervention of supernal love, gaining the discernment to tell truth from mere intelligence is certainly one key to psychological emancipation.

The company of poets

Poets occupy a unique place in Dante's mythic world. In the genre of epic poetry that Dante inherits, the poets take on the revered roles usually occupied by warriors or kings. They give key pieces of history or explanations. In the genre of religious allegory, poets take the roles usually reserved for martyrs and saints. And in Dante's personal narrative, his fellow poets bring joy and a palpable sense of relaxation as Dante engages them in lively conversations that would not have been out of place in a North Beach coffee house in the Beat era.

Virgil, whom Dante addresses as "my master," is a revered figure, one who offers Dante the highest form of instruction. But there are times when they seem more like fellows, exhausted or amazed together, two poets, who in life were separated by some 13 centuries, on a trek of discovery. When in Canto VI Virgil encounters the Troubadour poet Sordello, a fellow Mantuan, they embrace for several minutes and completely ignore Dante, who is not introduced until the next canto. And Virgil seems all too glad to cede some of the theological and metaphysical heavy lifting to his fellow Latin poet Statius, who accompanies them from Canto XXII onward. Tellingly, though, when Statius, tipped off by Dante to Virgil's identity, tries to embrace his knees, Virgil waves him off, as if to say, "Now that we are shades, we are all equal."

It is this sense of equality among poets that I think forms the basis for the twinship selfobject transference Dante forms with them. In Canto XXVI, just before Dante is to pass through the wall of flame, he encounters two of his most beloved fellow poets, Guido Guinizelli and the Troubadour poet Arnaut Daniel. With his two near-contemporaries, he engages in a bit of shop talk about the invention of "the sweet new style" of vernacular poetry, an invention to which Dante's own contributions are paramount. To Daniel, he pays the high honor of letting him enter the poem in his own Provencal language.

The matrix of Dante's transformation of the selfobject-surround is worth noting. A longed-for, idealized female has become a secret protector and the source of his spiritual renewal. A great poetic master, from whom Dante takes his form and some of the substance of his life's work, becomes a daily presence in his journey, instructing him as he urges Dante onward. Meetings with a cohort of cherished fellow poets, some of whom he knew personally, some only through their work, become a recurring refrain when Dante's energy flags or things get intense. They offer encouragement, gossip, instruction. Dante has dramatized a world that will meet his deepest needs. A guide, a purpose, a cohort. *This is what a self in trouble needs*, Dante is telling us. This and the inspiration, courage and creativity to imagine it into existence.

With this understanding of the psychological underpinnings of his journey, I will turn now to four important moments in the *Purgatorio* narrative. In Canto XVII, Virgil gives Dante a discourse on love; in Canto XXVII, Dante passes through a wall of flame; in Cantos XXX–XXXIII, Virgil leaves and crowns Dante with a blessing of autonomy; and in Canto XXX, Beatrice takes over as Dante's guide. Each marks a significant development in the healing narrative: the gaining of a new understanding of Dante's underlying motivations, the letting go of inhibiting fear and the termination-like experience in which the guide departs and Dante is crowned with a blessing of autonomy. Tellingly, this last moment is also the moment when he is reunited with his beloved Beatrice.

No creature is without love: the metapsychology of the *Purgatorio*

Heinz Kohut (1984) described the psychotherapy process as having two phases, understanding and explaining. Explaining supports and consolidates the gains made by the patient through the experience of feeling understood. Didactic passages appear throughout the *Commedia*, but at times they take on a greater importance. One example is in Canto XVII. While they are leaving the realm of the angry and standing just outside the realm of sloth, Virgil delivers to Dante a discourse on the nature of love. Medieval, scholastic and besotted with Aquinas, it is the kind of thing the casual reader of the *Purgatorio* might be tempted to skim. But it bears a closer look. The message it delivers – that all of the sins we witness in Purgatory are motivated (in however perverted a way) by love – is central to Dante's spiritual and psychological growth. By extension, it is central to our search for useful analogies between the *Purgatorio* and psychotherapy.

Since they are near nightfall, when all progress up Mount Purgatory is stopped, Virgil invites Dante to "gather some good fruit from our delay" (XVII:90, p. 167). Love, he explains, is the universal force of the creation: "Neither Creator nor creature ever/. . . was without love" (XVII:91–92, p. 167). He then describes two types of love, natural and mental. "The natural is always without error/but the other can err by choosing the wrong object/or having too much or too little vigor" (XVII:94–96, p. 167). This distinction between natural and mental love bears some resemblance to Winnicott's (1965) distinction between the true and false selves. And, as we shall see in the next chapter, it resembles William Blake's idea that consciousness evolves through different states, from innocence through experience to a state he calls "higher innocence."

The idea that it is love that underlies all motivation points to an argument that echoes down to our day and lies at the heart of psychoanalysis. Freud at first agreed with Aquinas/Virgil and saw all drives as forms of Eros. But later he added the concept of Thanatos, or a death instinct, to his drive theory. Kohut rejected drives altogether, seeing our psychological life as organized by the longing for stabilizing selfobjects or by defenses against the frustration of that longing. Freud's later theory would seem to rule over the *Inferno*, while the *Purgatorio* marks a more Kohutian turn.

Understanding a patient's problems as stemming from choosing the wrong object or having too much or too little vigor in the pursuit of that object would certainly mark a moment in therapy when shame and self-loathing might begin to be replaced by empathy and self-compassion. This is true as well for Dante, whose problems can now be understood as based in error rather than innate badness: "Thus you can understand that love must be/the seed in you of every virtue and/of every act that deserves punishment" (XVII:103–105, p. 169). This is what psychotherapists refer to as a *reframe*, a consideration of an action or characteristic in a new light or context. Kohut (1984) described traditional Freudian analysis as a kind of psychoeducation project in which the patient was led to acknowledge, and presumably tame, the terrible drives and urges (e.g., to kill one's father and marry one's mother) that lie buried in the unconscious.

By contrast, Virgil describes three forms of love's perversion – which amount to envy, the need to maintain power and shame – in which love "pursues the good in a corrupted way" (XVII:126, p. 169). Sloth is the sin of too little zeal, gluttony the sin of too much. From time to time, as Dante's soul becomes more enlightened, an angel removes one of the *P*'s (for *peccata*, or vice) that had been carved onto Dante's forehead at the beginning of his journey. This is accompanied by a feeling in Dante of lightness, of greater freedom. You can sometimes feel something analogous in psychotherapy, when a correct interpretation or mutually arrived-at understanding removes some of the weight of a patient's shame or guilt.

Through a wall of fire

Much of what happens in psychotherapy is undramatic. Small increments of mutual understanding, accretions of psychological structure like the invisible growth of a coral reef. This makes the therapy process hard to portray in movies or literature. The depictions often seem arch or over-wrought. That said, there are particular moments in therapy that mark a breakthrough. The Boston Change Process Group (2010) identifies these as moments of powerful connection and shared understanding between patient and therapist. Other theorists, such as Diana Fosha (2000), focus on the intensity of the affect expressed at such moments.

Epic and allegorical poetry are not limited by the need for such verisimilitude, but the climax of the *Purgatorio* – in which Dante and Virgil pass through a purifying wall of flame and enter the Earthly Paradise – feels true and natural, though it depicts a mythic event. We note Dante's brevity: the act of passing through the wall of flame occupies 18 lines. There are in fact three protagonists before the wall of flame, for Statius is still with him and Virgil. Statius and Virgil offer to go through first; then Virgil urges Dante onward with a parent-like strategy: "'Well/do you want to stay on this side?' and then [he] smiled/as at a child who has been won with an apple" (XXVII:43–45, p. 265). Virgil and Statius appeal to the motivation that underlies the whole journey: reuniting with Beatrice, who, they say, is waiting on the other side. Virgil tells Dante, "I seem to see her eyes already" (XXVII:54, p. 265). But as to the agony of the flame, Dante does not spare us: "As soon as I was in it I would have thrown/myself into boiling glass to be cooler/the burning there was so beyond measure" (XXVII:49–51, p. 265).

Here is a poem by poet and psychotherapist Anita Barrows that evokes the transformative power of this passage:

Questo Muro

Quando mi vide star pur fermo e duro/turbato un poco disse: "Or vedi figlio:/tra Beatrice e te e questo muro."

(When he saw me standing there unmoving, he was a bit disturbed and said, "No look, son, between Beatrice and you there is this wall.")
– Dante, *Purgatorio* XXVII

You will come at a turning of the trail
to a wall of flame

After the hard climb & the exhausted dreaming

you will come to a place where he
with whom you have walked this far
will stop, will stand
beside you on the treacherous steep path
& stare as you shiver at the moving wall, the flame

that blocks your vision of what
comes after. And that one
who you thought would accompany you always,
who held your face

tenderly a little while in his hands –
who pressed the palms of his hands into drenched grass
& washed from your cheeks the soot, the tear-tracks –

he is telling you now
that all that stands between you
& everything you have known since the beginning

is this: this wall. Between yourself
& the beloved, between yourself & your joy,
the riverbank swaying with wildflowers, the shaft

of sunlight on the rock, the song.
Will you pass through it now, will you let it consume

whatever solidness this is
you call your life, & send
you out, a tremor of heat,

a radiance, a changed
flickering thing?

(Barrows, 2016, p. 11)

Virgil cajoles, reasons and leads by example to get Dante to enter the flame. His simile of a parent with an apple is apt, for in all these actions, he is parental, and Dante is as a child. From the other side of the flame, though, the appeals are to an adult: a paean sung by angels, the possibility of seeing Beatrice's eyes. There are many religious and allegorical interpretations to the passage through flame, but at the relational level, it marks the moment when Dante moves from a child-like state of dependency into full adulthood and autonomy. Beyond the flame, Virgil will speak his last words to Dante, his famous blessing, "I crown and mitre you over yourself." Transformation and termination compressed into a single sequence.

Virgil departs: the blessing of autonomy

As we recall from Chapter 1, form in psychoanalysis is a mixture of received and emergent elements. Rarely are moments of breakthrough marked by acts of ritual or even celebration. One exception perhaps is termination, which in many treatments is announced, undergone and formally marked. The climactic moments of *Purgatorio* XXVII that we have been examining have both formal elements and elements that seem to have emerged out of Dante's imagination. The wall of purifying flame that marks the entrance to the Earthly Paradise is an example of the former, while Virgil's valedictory speech to Dante is an example of the latter. This sense of the known and the new underlies the best of analytic treatments. The patient feels that he is on a known path, that he is one of the many who have undergone analysis. And he feels that each moment of the treatment is unique to him and his therapist. Here is Virgil's speech:

> "You have seen the temporal fire
> and the eternal, my son, and you have come
> to where I, by myself, can see no farther.
> I have brought you here with understanding
> and art. From here on your own pleasure must guide you."

After bidding Dante to explore and enjoy the miraculous garden until his reunion with Beatrice, Virgil concludes:

> "Expect no further word or sign from me.
> your own will is whole, upright, and free,
> and it would be wrong not to do as it bids you.
>
> Therefore I crown and mitre you over yourself."
> (XXVIII:127–142, pp. 270–271)

I have noticed that I am often much more active in the beginning stages of therapy then at the end. The moment when a patient begins making his own interpretations, especially genetic interpretations, marks a turning toward this phenomenon. More and more, the patient becomes his own authority; the therapist is there to witness. The therapist is saying, in effect, you can trust your own impulses and desires now; they represent more of your true self. In Dante's words, they are organized more by natural than by mental love. Any paraphrase of the exquisite "Lord of yourself, I crown and mitre you," would be reductive: the words redound over 700 years and bring us to the edge of tears. Dante is now beyond Virgil's discernment. The therapist's mind and art are directed toward liberating the patient from the shackles of the past. As to the future: he must let him go with the blessing of being his own king rather than pledging fealty to another.

The reunion with Beatrice

As climactic as Virgil's final speech is, we still have six cantos to go, including Canto XXX, in which Virgil, still physically present though silent, disappears, and Beatrice announces herself by calling out Dante's name. The curious gender reversal that underlies much of the *Purgatorio* reaches its height in the last cantos. Virgil is more the tender and attentive maternal figure, Beatrice unavailable and scolding, like a contemporary father figure.

Beatrice speaks for the first time at the very moment Virgil disappears. For the first and only time in the *Commedia*, Dante hears his name called. "Dante, because Virgil leaves you/do not weep yet" (XXX:55–56, p. 295). The poet Dante's final tribute to his master, having Dante the character turn toward Virgil as a child would turn toward its mother, echoes the description of Aeneas reaching for his father in Book VI of the *Aeneid*. Dante writes, "But Virgil had left us, he was no longer there/among us, Virgil, most tender father,/Virgil to whom I gave myself to save me" (XXX:49–51, p. 295). In Dante's Italian, Virgil's name is repeated three times, invoking the magic number that secretly organizes so much of the cantos.

As though the baton had been passed, Beatrice now takes over Dante's instruction. But rather than being the expected comforter for his terrible loss, her voice is harsh. She warns him that "soon another wound/shall make you weep far hotter tears than those." In the guise of hearing his confession, she is about to give him a country scolding. And the gender bending continues, with Beatrice high on a chariot being compared to an admiral, inspecting his ships.

Like a husband who finds that once the honeymoon is over, his wife is after him about his bad habits, Dante finds Beatrice in no mood for cuddling or small talk. She forces him to see his ego-driven, selfish ways. The quest for love is the great developmental force that leads us to find relationship. But having love, being in a relationship, brings us face to face with our faults and limitations and that completes our human development. The world beyond Purgatory that Dante is in now is not some copacetic paradise. His empathic self psychology–oriented Virgil has been replaced, as it were, by a confrontative Freudian. And the pageant Dante witnesses in Canto XXXII depicts a giant and a whore fornicating, symbols of a corrupt church and politicians.

In order to give our patients what they need to develop, we must indeed become shape-shifters, masculine and feminine, supportive and confrontational. Our modern view of analysis has rejected the preplanned and formulaic. Though surprising, the fact that Dante arrives at the edge of Paradise only to find that his idealized Beatrice has turned into a lacerating Old Testament prophet feels true to life. And then, just when he needs respite from the terrible mother, he finds himself across the Lethe, the river of forgetfulness, in the arms of another maternal figure, Matilde, who is not identified in the text but seems a stark contrast to the Beatrice he has just encountered. Another triplet: kind Virgil, confrontative Beatrice, comforting Matilde. Three beats, three modes, three incarnations of therapist and patient. Till we arrive, at last, in the last words of the *Purgatorio*,

> made new again, when their leaves are new
> pure and ready to ascend to the stars.
> (XXXIII:144–145, p. 331)

Case vignette

For patients who suffer from posttraumatic stress disorder, descent to hell is a constant possibility. William's childhood as an only child in the care of a mother who suffered from severe bipolar disorder presented a sequence of hellish episodes that ended in her violent suicide when William was 18. There were times when his mother treated him like her only friend: they had adult conversations and watched the news together. And there were times when she would get manic and chase him around the house with a butcher knife.

Soon after beginning treatment, William suffered a second trauma: his longtime girlfriend broke up with him, revealing that during a brief and – he thought – trial separation, she had met someone else and was intending to get married. This plunged William into a catastrophic, at times near-psychotic, depression. He emerged shaken, convinced that he could not trust anything in the world to be what it seemed. He had a recurrent fear that I was going to betray him as well. He was sure that at any time, I would tell him that he was too much for me, that I was going to stop the treatment.

This fear-based side of the transference bore little resemblance to Dante's with Virgil. But at other times, he did view me as a revered expert.

He would bring a spiral-bound notebook to sessions and carefully write down my interpretations. For a long time, he persisted in believing that I was guiding him toward some cure according to a prescribed plan, an understandable wish for the rational basis to life that was so lacking in his childhood. He thought I was just being modest when I told him we were learning what he might need as we went along.

Another resemblance to Dante and Virgil is the way William constantly sought to establish a twinship relationship with me. He would probe for pieces of my personal history that were similar to his. Though he worked in a trade, he had graduated Phi Beta Kappa from a prestigious university and often would engage me in discussions of books and politics. We both loved Bob Dylan, and that was important to him. When I revealed to him that I grew up in a working-class background like his, he found this very important and comforting. When he found out I was Jewish, he made many comparisons between his traumatic experience and my relationship to the Holocaust.

William, bereft of the love of both his mother and of his girlfriend, needed a Virgil who would explain the way his memories haunted him and guide him through the underground terrain of the hells that would open in the face of posttraumatic triggers. He needed my hand to hold in the darkness, and he needed me to be a working-class, intellectual, Dylan-loving twin who, on account of the Jewish experience of the Holocaust, understood trauma.

Somewhere around the fourth or fifth year of treatment, it seemed we began to emerge from the Inferno into the daylight of Purgatory. My interpretative activity lessened. William would make his own forays into memory without prodding. He began on his own to make connections between past traumatic experience and current patterns of behavior.

In a series of sessions, William described what it had been like to come home from school. He always dreaded what he might find when he opened the door. He said he could almost "read" the house from the walkway. He would be somewhat prepared by the time he got to the front door and would know instantly from the light and the energy in the house what kind of a state his mother might be in. If it were bad, he would linger in his room for as long as he thought possible before going out. After a series of these recollections, he said, "I guess you can tell where my constant hypervigilance comes from. Not to mention my holing up all the time in bed in my apartment with a book and my cat." During this period, William grew more able to break the hold of "psychic equivalence" (Fonagy et al., 2002) – if I feel it, it must be real – and describe his fears as relating to a state of his own mind rather than seeing them as indicators of outside reality.

We both knew his increasingly vivid childhood recollections would inevitably lead to a description of the day he came home from high school to find the house surrounded by police, an ambulance and neighbors. Here it was, though the details become a bit blurred, as if still protected by a veil of dissociation. How did the neighbors react? He couldn't exactly say, though he clearly remembers being too ashamed to go into town for months afterward.

One vivid memory: he remembers being alone with his father after the crowd cleared out. His father was a solid man, intelligent though limited by his eighth-grade education, and mostly powerless to protect William from his mother's madness. On this night, though, he was like Virgil urging Dante through a wall of fire. "He put his hand on my shoulder and looked me in the eye. He said, 'We need to sleep here tonight. If we do not go in now, we'll never be able to go into this house again.' That night we slept in my room, side by side."

Winnicott's (1965) notion of the holding environment applies particularly to patients like William. Much of what I did was just "hold" him when he was triggered, or, more frequently, when he was sure he was about to be triggered. But therapists have needs as well, and a work of art like the *Commedia*, its elaborate formal structure interlaced with inventiveness, can provide a holding. Dante's is a work of radical self-invention, dizzying in the way it appropriates the details of his own inner life, history, literature, myth and religion. A precursor, perhaps, to the psychoanalytic project writ large. But beyond its audacity, its strength lies in its attention to the tiniest, heartbreaking details:

> When we had come to a place where the dew
> fends off the sun, there where it dries
> hardly at all because of the sea breeze
>
> my master spread out both his hands and laid them
> gently upon the grass, and I who
> understood what he intended to do
>
> leaned toward him my cheeks with their tear stains
> and he made visible again
> all that color of mine which Hell had hidden.
>
> (I:121–129, p. 9)

Chapter 8

Mind-forg'd manacles

William Blake and the emancipation
of consciousness

In every cry of every Man,
In every Infants cry of fear,
In every voice: in every ban,
The mind-forg'd manacles I hear.
    (Blake, 1970, "London," p. 27)

As a poet who set out to reshape human consciousness by removing the "mind-forg'd manacles" that trap us in a world of "woe" and "weakness" ("London," p. 27), William Blake lines up well with the therapy process. His diagnosis is that we have internalized pathological structures that lead us to blame ourselves and limit our potential. As a result, we are doomed to endless cycles of repetition in which our hopes are continually dashed and reborn. His treatment plan is a massive reframe in which we come to see ourselves as the creators of a new reality not prisoners of the old. His poetry fosters the development of what is now called *mentalization,* a theory of mind that acknowledges the subjective nature of reality and realizes there are other equally valid or even better ways to see the world. As in good therapy, Blake helps the integration of unknown or disavowed states of mind by teaching us to look beyond the manifest to an imaginative world in which our thoughts connect to larger themes of human experience. And perhaps most importantly, Blake's poems teach us that no matter how dire our straits or powerful our oppressors, change is possible in an instant.

Blake is a poet of such depth and complexity that his work, almost 300 years after his death, is still being explicated. Reading Blake is like listening to a challenging but rewarding patient. There are flashes of immediate meaning and gratification and hints of untold depths. Where Dante invoked Virgil as his guide and inspiration, Blake, who considered Dante one of his great heroes and poetic forefathers, takes up Dante's project of emancipation through an act of poetic self-invention. For Dante, this involves a hero's journey that begins in error, traverses the depth of human depravity and climbs toward the truth.

But truth and error coexist in a single moment for Blake, and each is defined by a mode of perception. "If the doors of perception were cleansed," he famously wrote in "The Marriage of Heaven and Hell" (1970, p. 39), "every thing would appear to man as it is, Infinite. For man has closed himself up, till he sees all things thro' narrow chinks of his cavern." Inspiration and imagination rather than arduous expiation are the Blakean keys to liberation. And the enemies of that liberation are the authority of the church and state, the oppression of an unjust economic system and the dominance of the Enlightenment's mechanistic worldview, sentiments that in many ways draw from Dante's savage satire of papal and temporal corruption.

Overview

Blake (1757–1827) was largely unknown – or worse, considered mad – in his own lifetime. He was a working-class man who, after apprenticing to an engraver at 14 and enrolling some seven years later at the Royal Academy of Art, set up his own print shop, where in addition to his commissions he produced illustrated editions of his own poetry, each plate heavy with commentary. Caught up in the political ferment of his times (indeed, at one point participating in an assault on a prison), Blake also produced radical pamphlets: his views have been identified as feminist and pro–sexual freedom. As a religious freethinker, he was anti-clergy and tended toward radical views of direct religious experience. One of his influences was the Swedish theologian Emanuel Swedenborg.

A few of Blake's short lyrics gained some early popularity, but they were largely misunderstood. A passage from his long poem, "Milton," "And did these feet in ancient time," was turned into an Anglican hymn. Given Blake's dismal view of the church and his championing of personal experience over doctrine, this remains a great irony. His work consists of aphorisms, short lyrics and longer "prophetic books," which depict a complex personal mythology. William Butler Yeats was one of Blake's champions and is responsible for his resurgent popularity in the 20th century. The prophetic books were not understood until critics like S. Foster Damon (1979) began to decipher them. Northrup Frye (1990b) was one of the first to see the consistency between his early lyrics and the later prophetic books. Many of Blake's best-known poems were discovered in notebooks after his death.

Joy and woe

By way of entry into William Blake's poetic project, let's look at a quatrain from his poem "Auguries of Innocence":

> Joy and Woe are woven fine
> A clothing for the soul divine
> Under every grief and pine
> Runs a joy with silken twine.
> (1970, p. 482)

At first pass, the quatrain seems to affirm a basic tenet of psychotherapy – that the way to recover joy is to go deeply into grief. Theorists like Diana Fosha (2000), for example, define completing a feeling of woe or grief as the very essence of the therapy process. The geological metaphor Blake presents in line 3 of the poem – that feelings are arranged in layers, the truer or purer ones lying below the more recently experienced – is familiar to therapists, most of whom would be comfortable with the idea that therapy proceeds by following a valuable thread through a patient's discourse that yields unforeseen connections.

But Blake's poems contain another layer of meaning beneath the manifest. Joy and woe are woven fine, as if they are indeed deeply connected. But they are woven into clothes that cover or obscure the soul; they are not part of the soul itself. There is a sense here, as in all of Blake, that seeming opposites like joy and woe are in dialectical relationship, that one implies the other. "Without contraries there is no progression," he writes in "The Marriage of Heaven and Hell" (p. 34). While it is clear that going into sorrow helps us reach joy, it is less clear whether the silken twine that connects the two is the source of liberation or the tie that binds us to an endless cycle. If the latter, then Blake's project is to break that cycle, even if it means severing the silken threads of emotional attachment that hold back our evolution. Speaking of man's fallen state in his prophetic book, "Milton," Blake hopes to help man "cast off the rotten rags of memory by Inspiration," and "To take off his filthy garments & clothe him with Imagination" (p. 141).

Another example of Blake's layering of meanings may be useful. Blake's illustration of his poems often supply a bit of irony. The savage Tyger of his famous poem is more like a tame pussycat. The point, as always in Blake, is to emphasize that perception is everything. Near the end of his life, Blake created a series of engravings and paintings to illustrate Dante's *Commedia*. "The Giant and the Harlot" depicts a scene from *Purgatorio* XXII in which Dante views the full range of human corruption on parade, including a float satirizing the monstrous fornication of a corrupt pope and a debauched emperor. But in Blake's painting, the two look more like actors in a B-movie poster, and the serpent who wraps his tail around them looks more frightened than frightening. Here Blake gives us a satirical reading of a satirical passage: saying in effect that it is not only the church and state that are in error but our way of looking at them. Evil is not (or not only) an external force; it originates in an error of perception, an error of consciousness that makes us the slave of fierce tygers and debauched popes rather than their imaginative master.

Blake's thinking is influenced by the Gnostic tradition that holds that the world we see is but a shell or fallen edifice concealing the truth within. His own version of the "gnostic gospels" reveals an alternative view of both the Bible and history. We can imagine that he would have delighted in a book like Freud's *Moses and Monotheism*, which presents a psychoanalytic reading of the Old Testament.

Blake, psychoanalysis and the project of liberation

In contrast to Dante, Blake's complicated oeuvre, which includes deceptively simple lyrics and dense epics filled with complex personal mythology, does not describe a road trip from hell up to heaven. Blake's hell, which he called *Ulro*, is the post-Enlightenment world around us. It overvalues reason (which Freud would have called the ego) and undervalues energy (Freud's id). Our psyches in Blake are fully contextualized, embedded in corrupt social systems and hypocritical religious institutions. He identified with the American and French Revolutions but felt they failed because they did not go far enough toward defining a new form of consciousness.

The contrary states that Blake describes, which he called Innocence and Experience, imply each other and together dialectically imply a progression toward a state that Blake called "Higher Innocence." There are analogies between this progression of consciousness and the psychotherapy process. The dichotomies of Innocence and Experience, unconscious and conscious, good and evil, energy and reason bear some analogy to the intrapsychic conflicts Freud described as well as to the stages of child psychic development Klein wrote of. For Klein, like Dante, progress happens in developmental stages. Her depressive position roughly corresponds to Blake's state of "experience." Freud, like Blake, saw the inevitable conflict between unconscious drives and conscious intentions as optimally resulting in a third term. For Freud, this was a moral, observing part of the self that helped resolve or at least neutralize the conflict. For Blake the third term, imagination, provides transcendence. Blake would agree with Stevens: "The world imagined is the ultimate good" (Stevens, 1978, p. 524).

A century after Blake, psychoanalysis took up the question of human unhappiness. Where Blake had written, "Sooner murder an infant in its cradle then nurse unacted desires" (p. 37), Freud viewed our drives and their repression as a needed and inevitable dialectic. At least in its earliest iterations, Freud's psychoanalysis can be read as a reaction to the Romantic movement in general and to Germanic Idealism in particular. Freud read history not as a progression but as a perpetual struggle between conscious intention and unconscious urges. Blake was inspired by the American and French Revolutions; Freud (at least from 1917 on) was appalled by World War I and the rise of fascism.

But this contrast may be more apparent than real. Blake was against the Enlightenment's valorization of pure reason, not reason itself, which he viewed as the outward bound that gave pure energy its shape and form. And Freud found a home in the human psyche for the dark energies that the Greeks called *chthonic*. The psychoanalytic project involved our acknowledging rather than denying their power. In the 60s, both Blake and Freud were rebranded. Herbert Marcuse (1955), among others, mixed psychoanalysis and Marxism into a liberation philosophy. And writers like Aldous Huxley and Allen Ginsberg, along with rock stars like Jim Morrison and Patti Smith, found in Blake a model for a psychedelic revolution.

In the 50 years that followed, psychoanalysis, at least in fits and starts, has continued its affiliation with liberation. Winnicott (2016) argued against the imposition of a requirement of falseness and conformity to others' needs in human development. Bernard Brandchaft (Brandchaft, Doctors, and Sorter, 2010) saw the job of psychoanalysis as emancipating the patient from "Pathological Structures of Accommodation." Aron and Starr (2013) have advocated turning psychoanalytically based treatment into a movement that aligns itself with the needs and strivings of working- and middle-class patients.

Meanwhile, Blake emerges as a subtle and often ironic critic of human consciousness whose own views do not exactly reside in the speakers of his poems, whether they be poor chimney sweeps or Satan himself. We approach Blake, as we approach our patients, by deeply listening and by embracing rather than overriding their apparent contradictions. What we find in Blake's poems is an elucidation of the levels of human consciousness and a project for its imaginative redemption. In order to understand this project, we will follow his elucidation of the states of human consciousness through Innocence to Experience to hints at a level Blake called variously "Beulah," "Eden" or "Higher Innocence."

We track our patients not only for content and affect but also thematically. Is their thematic material based on the repetition of old hurts and traumas, or does it show hopes and longings for a new, corrective experience? Is the material we are listening to themed with envy, rivalry and assertion, or is it themed with longings for comfort and understanding? In the background, we have some developmental map or schema we are referring to. So too does Blake. His poems refer to differing states of consciousness and constantly create ironies between the reader, the speaker and the poet.

Songs of Innocence

Dante's journey is linear in the *Commedia*; Hell, Purgatory and Heaven are geographically separate. Sin, redemption and transcendence are moshed up in Blake's *Songs* – like an optical illusion that one minute looks like a sailboat and the next minute a rabbit – which we see is a matter of perception and point of view. Reading the *Songs* invokes the kind of multivalent listening of the analyst, who combines cognitive, affective and associative elements. "Would you be jealous if I fell in love with somebody?" a female patient asks. "I'd be happy for you," the therapist responds, or alternatively, "Maybe a little." Are we listening to her affect, to our sense of what she needs to hear or to our own associations? "Little lamb who made thee/Dost thou know who made thee" Blake asks at the beginning of the *Songs of Innocence* (p. 8). The same question twice, to different effect. The repetition moves our attention from fact to a theory of mind. Does he know? Do we know? Does the poet know who made this lamb, bleating creature and religious symbol?

Our study of the poems of childhood in Chapter 3, with their juxtaposition of two different states of consciousness – that of the child and that of the parent – prepared us for this. These two contrasting points of view correspond to states of Innocence and Experience in Blake. The frontispiece of Blake's engraved edition of the *Songs of Innocence and Experience* describes them as "Shewing the Two Contrary States of the Human Soul." As the critic Robert Gleckner (1966) writes, "Blake employed a central group of related symbols to form a dominant, symbolic pattern; his are the child, the father and Christ, representing the states of innocence, experience and a higher innocence" (p. 9). From a psychoanalytic point of view, the state of Innocence corresponds to the preoedipal world of mother and infant; the state of Experience corresponds to the triangulating entrance of the father-rival. Higher Innocence, in the secular analytic view, would be the reclaiming of vitality and initiative gained from resolution of the oedipal rivalry.

As Gleckner points out, "For the serious reader of Blake's *Songs* . . . a constant awareness of the context or state in which a poem appears is indispensable" (1966, p. 10). Again, an analogy to analysis is illuminating: the patient/speaker speaks without knowledge of his unconscious motivations or meanings; the analyst/reader listens from his broader understanding of human consciousness. And these contexts of speaker and reader are themselves continuously evolving within the ongoing series of poems Blake presents. In this sense, the collection of *Songs of Innocence and Experience* do form a kind of Dante-esque narrative progression. Even in the earliest poems, the speaker and the reader exist in different contexts, but as the poems progress, the speakers become increasingly split off from their own reality, and innocence gives way to a kind of denial. Reality is now the province of the reader, in ironic contrast to the world the speaker describes.

Let's begin. In the first poem following the "Introduction" to *Songs of Innocence*, "The Shepherd" (p. 7). It is only the reader's knowledge of wolves that contextualizes the pure joy of the Shepherd:

How sweet is the shepherd's sweet lot!
From the morn to the evening he strays;
He shall follow his sheep all the day,
And his tongue shall be filled with praise.

For he hears the lambs' innocent call,
And he hears the ewes' tender reply;
He is watchful while they are in peace,
For they know when their shepherd is nigh.

Here at the beginning of the *Songs*, the juxtaposition of the differing contexts is not satirical: the pure pastoral world they evoke is a legitimate imaginative state, a foundation of lyric poetry from Biblical, Greek and Christian (e.g., the Lamb of God) sources. The nontraumatized infant *is* watched over by the shepherd/mother. The call and reply of ewe and lamb evoke for us the intricate dialogue of mothers and infants revealed in Beatrice Beebe's stop-motion split-screen studies (Beebe, Cohen, and Lachmann, 2016). "Come and lick/My white neck," Blake writes with exquisite tenderness in "Spring" (p. 15).

But already in the second stanza of "The Shepherd," the boy-shepherd figure has morphed from a state of child-like (or lamb-like) joy into a separate state of mind, a state of watchfulness. He knows of danger, so he provides peace and security. The shepherd becomes a symbol of the watchful Christ. At the very beginning of the cycle, child-like joy is linked to the end-state Higher Innocence of Christ consciousness. But this seems almost too pat. There is no tension, no development. The danger here is falling into a kind of regressive nostalgia. We see it in patients who seem unwilling or unable to accurately locate the source of their childhood traumas, who insist on seeing their childhoods as happy and their parents as good shepherds.

Even if we begin in a pastoral heaven, we don't stay there long. No one in these early poems is crowned and mitred over themselves. In "Night" (p. 13), the shepherd/boy/mothers stand and weep rather than protect the innocent victims from "wolves and tygers": "But if they rush dreadful/the angels most heedful/Receive each mild spirit/New worlds to inherit." Blake, as always, is working at different levels simultaneously. New worlds to inherit seem cold comfort for being eaten. And the Angels merely carry the victims up to heaven; they do not protect them. Is this a kind of false transcendence, a "flight to health" as we say of patients who rush to get better so they can avoid their real pain? "The lions ruddy eyes/ shall flow with tears of gold," Blake writes. Really? By the last stanza, the fierce lion has become a Christ/shepherd figure who "wash'd in life's river,/My bright mane for ever/Shall shine like the gold/As I guard o'er the fold." These simple-seeming poems present a complex iconography of predators, prey and protectors. Who is who, and what has happened? At this point in the *Songs*, we can't know yet. Why, mysteriously, is the robin in "The Blossom" sobbing? Sobbing robins and lions acting as shepherds: we are in a world similar to the beginning of a treatment when we are not sure who is who or what is what. But soon enough, a world of trauma and violation begins to emerge.

As they enter the phase in which their trauma histories emerge, our patients often seem to ask, "Is there a meaning to trauma? Is suffering redemptive?" Not necessarily, the *Songs of Innocence* suggest. What is redemptive is realizing the source of our trauma and overcoming the false meekness and identification with the oppressor that traumatized people display. By the end of the series, the *Songs of Innocence* deal with very traumatic material indeed – child labor and racism. The only thing inno-cent here is the speakers' naiveté or denial. For instance, take the poem "The Chimney Sweep" (p. 10) that appears in the *Songs of Innocence* and the *Songs of Experience*. In the first, the boy whose mother died in his infancy and whose father sold him into indentured servitude advises his fellow child sweeps, "if all do their duty, they need not fear harm." Touch-ing and cringe- worthy, in equal measure.

In "The Little Black Boy" (p. 9), the speaker shows his internalized racism: "My mother bore me in the southern wild,/And I am black, but O! my soul is white." The speaker thinks his blackness is a transitory state from which God's love will free him: "And we are put on earth a little space/That we may learn to bear the beams of love." Again, the Blakean multiplicity of meanings. When the black child speaker pro-poses a colorblind future, "When I from black and he from white cloud free/And round the tent of God like lambs we joy," we are moved. But when at poem's end he wants to "stroke his [white companion's] silver hair,/And be like him and he will then love me," his innocence approaches self-abasement. These poems correspond to cases in which the therapist alone holds the knowledge of the patient's trauma. I once had a case in which the knowledge of abuse remained at the margins the entire time, while the patient defended her abusive father and the mother who protected him.

Blake's inherent critique of Innocence as a form of consciousness is consonant with Freud and especially with Jung. Both saw a denial of darker thoughts and instincts as dangerous. Freud saw destructive energy as having its own set of drives, which must be accepted and neutralized. Jung believed that the repression of the Shadow was the source of our greatest malaise. But it would be a disservice if we only analyzed rather than listened to the *Songs of Innocence*. Blake's genius is that he can be both lyric and satirical at the same time, or at least in close proximity. These poems twist and dance: "Merrily Merrily we welcome in the Year" ("Spring," pp. 14–15), he writes. Blake means it when he says in the "Introduction" that he wrote "my happy songs" so "every child may joy to hear." We must have joy, he seems to be saying, even as we dispel our illusions.

Songs of Experience

"The Clod and the Pebble" (p. 18), the third poem in *Songs of Experience*, lays out Blake's notion of contrary states in a way that might seem familiar to therapists:

"Love seeketh not itself to please,
Nor for itself hath any care,
But for another gives its ease,
And builds a Heaven in Hell's despair."

So sung a little Clod of Clay
Trodden with the cattle's feet,
But a Pebble of the brook
Warbled out these metres meet:

"Love seeketh only self to please,
To bind another to its delight,
Joys in another's loss of ease,
And builds a Hell in Heaven's despite."

The pebble seems to be a perfect description of the narcissistic character type who would "bind another to its delight." The clod would seem to be the healthier, more evolved person. The therapist who could turn such a pebble into a loving, optimistic, healing clod would be a powerful clinician indeed. But this is Blake; there is another level of meaning.

In the middle stanza, the clod, already a more lowly symbol than the pebble, is denigrated, while the pebble seems exalted. Even the herd-bound cattle tread on the clod; the pebble is polished by the brook and sings tunefully. Given that we are in the realm of Experience, Blake suggests that innocence is a limited form of consciousness, the ground (here literally) from which Experience develops. There has long been a debate in psychoanalysis over the nature of narcissism: is it a derailment of normal development or a normal stage we (hopefully) pass through? Blake seems to be saying we need a pebble phase in which we are agentic in the destruction of our preoedipal heaven. (Here, we note, Blake seems quite Kleinian!) We might add too that Heaven and Hell do not merely represent good and evil in Blake's symbolic lexicon. Hell is energy; Heaven is reason, the outward bound of energy.

Little lyrics like "The Clod and the Pebble" aside, most of the *Songs of Experience* take us on a journey through an inferno equal to Dante's. Whereas Dante uses the myth of a voyage to the underworld as a means to satirize the above-ground world, Blake depicts the world immediately around him as hell. In the *Songs of Innocence*, the children, however abused, maintain their optimism. By the time we get to the *Songs of Experience*, they are crushed utterly, even prenatally, as in "London" (p. 27), where the children of prostitutes are infected with venereal disease. The paired poems are illuminating: in the *Innocence* version of "Holy Thursday" (p. 13), we wince to see the poor children paraded through the church before the "wise guardians of the poor," but a semblance of the children's innocence is maintained, and we are moved when they raise "their innocent hands" and sing. In the *Songs of Experience*, the children live in "eternal winter," "reduced to misery,/Fed with a cold and usurous hand" (p. 19). The concluding quatrain drips with sarcasm toward the Church, which affirms the lie that "Babe can never be hungry there/No poverty the mind appall." By a similar token, the children in the *Experience* version of the "Chimney Sweeper" (p. 22) cry "weep, weep, in notes of woe!" The delusion is now on the part of society: "And because I am happy & dance & sing/They think they have done me no injury."

An even more complex elucidation of fallen consciousness is offered in one of his most famous and simple-seeming poems, "Ah Sun-flower"(p. 26), which I offer here in its entirety:

Ah! Sun-flower, weary of time
Who countest the steps of the Sun:
Seeking after that sweet golden clime
Where the travellers journey is done.

Where the Youth pined away with desire,
And the pale Virgin shrouded in snow:
Arise from their graves and aspire,
Where my Sun-flower wishes to go.

We looked at this poem briefly in our discussion of sound and rhythm in Chapter 1. At first run-through, the poem repeats Blake's critique of sexual repression: the youth pining away with desire and the pale virgin freezing to death. "Break this heavy chain/That does my bones around/Selfish/vain/Eternal bane!/That free love with bondage bound" he writes in "Earth's Answer" (p. 18).

But the poem's critique of fallen consciousness runs deeper than a critique of sexual repression. Even a liberated sexuality keeps us in thrall to desire, bound to nature, bound to the body. In nature, we are trapped in time like the sunflower, tracking the sun's movement across the sky. Our deepest desires will never be filled in nature, only out of it, in the sweet golden clime of the imagination. If the natural world is all we have, Blake is saying, our unfulfilled desires will morph into a longing for death as a release from time.

Here Blake is at his most radical. No return to Innocence for him, no flower children parading in bell bottoms. And no longing for the Christian heaven beyond death, either, "Where the travellers journey is done." He wants a world of the imagination, a world of poetry: "When the sun rises, do you not see a round disc of fire somewhat like a guinea? Oh! no, no! I see an innumerable company of the heavenly host crying 'Holy, holy, holy is the Lord God Almighty!'" he writes in "A Vision of the Last Judgement" (1970, p. 555). One of the most famous Zen koans is "There is a ship in a bottle. How do we get the ship out of the bottle?" The answer is a shout: "HA!" A shock into awakening. It is a mental bottle the ship is in.

Without the imagination, we will cycle endlessly between states of Innocence and states of Experience.

Higher Innocence

Sprinkled all through the *Songs of Experience* are glimpses of another, higher state of consciousness. They are often marked by references to gold, the alchemical goal of all transformation. According to S. Foster Damon's *A Blake Dictionary* (1979), in Blake's lexicon gold is a symbol of our highest intellectual capacities. So the "sweet golden clime" of the "Sunflower" poem is not just an ironic symbol for our escapist desires; it is a product of the human imagination, which envisions a world of eternity and infinity out of a moment in time or a grain of sand in nature. "The Voice of the Ancient Bard" dwells in the level of experience, where fallen leaders "Wish to lead others where they should be led" (pp. 31–32). But the poem ends with the Bard (in Blake, the Bard is often used interchangeably with Christ) calling, "Youth of delight come hither/And see the opening morn/Image of truth new born." Again we see Blake use the image of the rising sun as a symbol of this new consciousness. The long vowels and slow rhythms of "Ah! Sun-flower, weary of time" give way in this poem toward the end of *Songs of Experience* to quick phrases and staccato rhythms: "Doubt is fled," "Dark disputes," "tangled roots" – full of energy and possibility.

"The Tyger" includes in the penultimate stanza the question, "Did he who made the lamb make thee?" which, depending upon your state of consciousness, might or might not be rhetorical. If the speaker is implying that the answer is no, then we are in the realm of contrary states, and Innocence and Experience will stay separate, without synthesis, and cycle endlessly. But if the question is rhetorical, then the answer is "of course," and we are moving toward a synthesis. Lamb and tyger merge in the world of the imagination, where opposing forces play against each other in an ongoing act of poetic creation.

The important question for Blake, and for our patients as well, is who "he" is, who is the creator? The creator of the material world of experience is Urizen (your reason), Blake's god of stony realism and of this material, time-bound world. His are the "stars" that in "The Tyger" "threw down their spears" that nail us to our fate. Although they may "water heaven with their tears," grief alone won't set us free.

But if the world we inhabit is one of imagination, created by the Bard, then the lamb and the tyger are part of a divine, creative synthesis. This synthesis is what Blake has in mind when he talks of Higher Innocence. Beyond an endless cycle of good and evil, heaven and hell, Innocence and Experience, the Bard imagines a world where the "Contraries" lead to an expansion of consciousness. Ultimately, Blake tells us, it is up to each of us to become the creator of our own world. Most therapists would consider a treatment successful if it helped a patient break out of self-defeating cycles and acquire a newfound sense of autonomy and empowerment, along with a renewed interest in their own creativity.

Breaking cycles

Much thinking in psychology and psychoanalysis has gone into identifying pathological cycles in which, for instance, trauma is replicated across generations. Mary Main and Erik Hesse's attachment research (1990), for instance, shows that a mother's own history of trauma predicts the child's disorganized attachment. Stolorow and his colleagues (1997) talk of a "bipolar transference" in which the patient's subjective experience oscillates between a hope for a longed-for new, developmentally needed experience and a repetition of old contexts that, though familiar, are retraumatizing. Mitchell (1995) emphasizes this oscillation in psychoanalytic treatment as well. We are all too familiar with patients' cycles of sobriety and relapse, mania and depression, family violence and reconciliation.

Blake's work is concerned with cycles as well. In his complicated mythology, characters are continuously morphing into their opposites. The youthful, rebellious figure Orc becomes the patriarchal ruler Urizen. The female figure Enitharmon, an earth-mother figure who represents beauty, morphs into Tirzah, a dominatrix/temptress figure who separates nations and sows strife. In his poem "The Mental Traveler" (pp. 475–477), a babe "born in joy" is captured by a "Woman old" who "nails him down upon a rock,/Catches his shrieks in cups of gold." The woman here could stand for a repressive society, which exploits the young for financial gain. His subjectivity, his very nervous system, is reduced to a thing:

> Her fingers number every Nerve
> Just as a miser counts his gold;
> She lives upon his shrieks and cries
> And she grows young as he grows old.

But in the next two stanzas, the cycle is reversed:

> Till he becomes a bleeding youth
> And She becomes a Virgin bright
> Then he rends up his Manacles
> And binds her down for his delight.
>
> He plants himself in all her Nerves,
> Just as a husbandman his mold;
> And she becomes his dwelling place
> And Garden fruitful seventy fold.

A feminist interpretation of this poem might be gleaned from reading backward what we have quoted so far: man subdues (e.g., rapes) the feminine natural world for his own profit, but ultimately this violence creates a violent, exploitive society that ends up subduing him. The important point is Blake's view of the endless cycles of struggle between the sexes, between young and old, between victim and victimizer. A psychoanalytic view of this might see an endless cycle of narcissism and trauma, in which the youthful energy of children is distorted into a series of false selves. The alternation between states of Innocence and a fallen world of Experience will continue unabated unless interrupted, Blake maintains, by a new imaginative reality.

Chariots of fire

Blake's most succinct statement of how we can interrupt these endless cycles through an act of imagination comes in one of his most famous passages, the one from his prophetic poem "Milton" (pp. 94–95) that we mentioned earlier as having been misunderstood as a patriotic Anglican hymn:

> And did these feet in ancient time
> Walk upon England's mountains green;
> And was the Holy Lamb of God
> On England's pleasant pastures seen?

The key to this poem is to see all its questions as rhetorical, implying yes. Although this poem sounds nationalistic, it is not. The first stanza invokes the state of Innocence. The second stanza, with its famous reference to "dark Satanic Mills," invokes Experience. Both are omnipresent, because they are mental states, states of consciousness.

> And did the Countenance Divine,
> Shine forth upon our clouded hills?
> And was Jerusalem builded here,
> Among these dark Satanic Mills?

Are the lamb and the Satanic Mills, Innocence and Experience, doomed to endless cycling, in the present as well as historically? The critical element here is understanding what Blake means by Jerusalem. Does he mean the historical city site of the First and Second Temples? At least from a historical perspective, the answer is no; it was "builded" in Palestine. But Jerusalem in Blake's symbolic world is the "Divine Vision in every individual," writes S. Foster Damon (1979). A vision that is equally at home in Lambeth, England, or, as I write this, in Berkeley, California.

Unlike a Buddhist notion of enlightenment, in which the mind is cleared to *receive* the truth about consciousness, Blake (1970, pp. 94–95) sees this transformation of consciousness as happening through "Mental Fight," a kind of spiritual warfare:

> Bring me my Bow of burning gold:
> Bring me my arrows of desire:
> Bring me my Spear: O clouds unfold!
> Bring me my Chariot of fire!
>
> I will not cease from Mental Fight
> Nor shall my sword sleep in my hand:
> Till we have built Jerusalem,
> In England's green & pleasant Land.

"O clouds unfold" could be Blake's motto, as well as that of psychoanalysis.

Blake is a poet of passionate engagement. He seeks not to transcend emotion but to harness his "arrows of desire" for a higher purpose. His idea of "Mental Fight" lines up well with Freud's conflict-based model of the psyche. Rather than escape these inevitable conflicts, we must seek to transform them. The conflict between merger with the object and self-delineation in Winnicott (1971a) is resolved through an act of imagination in "transitional space." For Freud, creativity is a product of our ability to sublimate our drives into a higher purpose. Blake's view of the imagination as the place where such conflicts can be resolved anticipated their views by more than a century.

For Blake, as Dante, poetry is the vehicle of liberation. While Dante's Paradise is largely a product of his own invention, he maintained the useful fiction that he was reporting, not creating. Blake's paradise is entirely *de novo*. It is not a static world at all but a world of intellectual and poetic "Mental Fight[s]" in which we battle to build an ever more perfect City, not on a hill but right here among our fields and dark Satanic Mills.

Or, for therapists, in the muted light of our consulting room. We turn to a case example in which an act of spiritual reimagination helped the patient heal from a life constrained by terrible childhood trauma.

Case example: Deirdre

"Our father did terrible things to us. He would come in our room at night. Especially when mother was having one of her times, or when she had left us."

"'Don't listen to her. She makes things up. What she doesn't want you to know is she has men over, for money. They pay her to fuck them.'"

"One time he took my pet rabbit out of its cage, and held it over a pot of boiling water. 'If you ever tell anyone, I'll boil your rabbit alive,' he said."

"My daddy, he isn't bad. He just needs me, because mother keeps talking so funny."

"I brought you something today, Dr. Shaddock. It's just a piece of paper, but it's my most important possession. I keep it with me everywhere. My mother wrote it one time when she wasn't crazy. Here, read it out loud."

"It says, 'Please believe my daughter. All the things she says happened to her really happened.'"

Though the case of Deirdre occurred near the beginning of my career as a psychoanalytically informed psychotherapist, it remains one of my most significant; one in which we were both changed forever.

Deirdre came to me with a six-session mandate from her employee assistance program. She stayed in treatment for almost 15 years, weekly at first, sporadically thereafter, paying a reduced fee or accessing her EAP benefits from her work as a tradeswoman for a local utility. I had had little training in working with severe abuse and trauma or in the treatment of what is now called dissociative identity disorder. What I did have was a natural affinity for her as a person and a commitment to hang in there with her. I never succeeded in getting Deirdre's subpersonalities to acknowledge or talk to one another.

It did not occur to me until I set out to write this chapter that my years of studying Blake, both at Berkeley (where one of my teachers was the magnificent Northrup Frye) and on my own later, might have helped me with this case. But my two most valuable assets – the ability to move without judgment between contradictory states of consciousness and the capacity never to lose hope that change was possible – could have been derived from Blake.

Deirdre's host personality could, I see now, have been a character in one of the *Songs of Innocence*. Dressed in overalls, hair tied in a scarf, she often expressed a kind of naïve wonder at the world, even as she told the most harrowing of stories from her childhood. She absolutely refused to blame either her schizophrenic mother or her to-me-psychopathic father for any of her troubles. Occasionally an even younger-seeming alter would show up, carrying a stuffed animal. And there were several provocatively dressed ones as well. These uniformly accused her of lying about her abuse and being man-crazed. "But most thro' midnight streets I hear/How the youthful Harlots curse/Blasts the newborn infants tear," Blake wrote in "London," nailing the intergenerational transmission of trauma. Innocence and Experience, alternating in my waiting room, with no hint of transcendence present.

The climax of the case took place outside of therapy. It involved a religious transformation of her consciousness that Blake might have approved of, despite his anticlerical stance. During one of our lowest points, Deirdre announced that she was out of money and needed to stop therapy. I offered to lower my fee down to practically zero, but she said that wouldn't be right. That was the last I heard from her for several years, during which time I found myself wondering if she was still alive. I had heard of patients quitting therapy to spare their therapist the trauma of their suicide. Then, out of the blue, she called to schedule an appointment.

"All those others who used to come in here," she told me, "they leave me alone. They're gone now. Something miraculous happened. I hope you believe me. My youngest brother Ted, he'd always been really mean to me and wouldn't even talk to me. But he got back into being a Catholic last year, and his priest told him he had to help me. So he took me to this kind of tent revival. I didn't even know that Catholics had such things. I told my brother I'd go, but I was going to sit in the back and just watch. He agreed not to make me say or do anything. So I was just sitting there, a little put off by it all to be honest, when the priest starts walking up to the back row toward me. He says, 'I can feel the presence of someone who thinks she is responsible for something, but she is not responsible, she is blameless.' And he stands over me and says, 'In the Name of Jesus Christ our Lord, let us pray that this woman is relieved of her suffering,' and the whole congregation is praying for me. And in truth I didn't feel anything overwhelming. I just felt really peaceful. But later I felt, almost physically, you know, the other personalities just leave me, just go off into the night, and they've never come back."

Deirdre's suffering didn't vanish, but her multiple personality disorder never returned. She became a very conservative Catholic. In a Blakean twist, she married a radical labor lawyer who had been a member of the Communist party. "His books of Marx on one wall, my picture of the Virgin on the other" was how she described it. For the last number of years, I saw Deirdre for her six EAP sessions each July. Then she called to say she had retired and was moving out of state.

Something I cannot claim to understand created a powerful and lasting transformation of Deirdre's consciousness "in the name of Jesus." I would like to think that Deirdre's ability to imagine another reality beyond the world of her suffering played a part in it. The poet who saw in an ordinary sunrise "an innumerable company of the heavenly host crying 'Holy, holy, holy is the Lord God Almighty'" would have approved.

Chapter 9

A universe between my hat and boots

Whitman's self as a model for empathic connection

> I pass death with the dying and birth with the new-washed babe, and am not contained between my hat and boots.
>
> (Whitman, 1983, p. 27)

Reading the poems of Walt Whitman can be helpful to therapists in two ways: for the heartfelt empathy his poems show for all the things in the world and for his expansive and complex view of the self. And out of these two flows a third, a moral imperative this intimate relationship with the world implies. As we shall see, the three are deeply connected. His sense of empathy flows from a self that is "large [and] contains multitudes" (Whitman, 1983, p. 72). In his early, unsurpassed masterpiece, "Song of Myself," shamanic Whitman journeys across a vast array of souls. His me is *we*, his we, *me*: "all men ever born are my brothers, and the women my sisters and lovers" (Whitman, 1983, p. 26). We witness the poet turn himself inside out, weaving with exquisite tenderness a relational bridge between the world outside and his own world:

> The runaway slave came to my house and stopt outside,
> I heard his motions cracking the twigs of the woodpile
> Through the swung half-door of the kitchen I saw him limpsy and weak,
> And went where he sat on a log and led him in and assured him,
> And brought water and fill'd a tub for his sweated body and bruis'd feet.
>
> (Whitman, 1983, pp. 29–30)

Whitman's self

Whitman writes in section 21 of "Song of Myself":

> I am the poet of the Body and I am the poet of the Soul,
> The pleasures of heaven are with me and the pains of hell are with me,
> The first I graft and increase upon myself, the latter I translate into a
>   new tongue.
>
>   (1983, p. 39)

His self is a crossroads through which all humanity, all of existence, passes. His mind is not isolated from his body, and both are exquisitely connected to the world. Stolorow and Atwood, writing in *Contexts of Being* (1992), describe the "myth of the isolated mind," in which "the individual exists separately from the world of physical nature and also from engagement with others" (p. 7). When Whitman writes "Walt Whitman, a kosmos" (1983, p. 41), it is clear that his model of the mind is the diametrical opposite of that isolation.

The poetic mind Whitman invokes in his early poetry is vaster than the isolated "Cartesian" one that Stolorow and Atwood describe. It is more akin to what we would call today a field or dynamic system. Whitman's consciousness expands as "my ties and ballasts leave me" (p. 49). This field, which is also his poem, comes to contain all of space and time. His mystical sense is not vague or airy; it is redolent with the smells and feels of actual people and actual things. It is said of Freud that he brought the gods down from Olympus and placed them in the human family. An analogous comment could be made of Whitman, that he brought his mystical vision of oneness down from the heavens and placed it in the human landscape he observed around him. Whitman's attention to details in that landscape resembles our analytic attention. And in his later poems, these details – Lincoln's hearse, a male goose calling for his mate – place his mystical vision in the context of human trauma. A newfound sorrow extends his remarkable poetic empathy.

I think it would behoove us as therapists to adopt a stance toward our patients like the one Whitman takes in this snippet from "Song of Myself":

> I am of the old and young, of the foolish as much as the wise
> Regardless of others, ever regardful of others,

Maternal as well as paternal, a child as well as a man
Stuffed with the stuff that is coarse, stuffed with the stuff that is fine.

(p. 40)

This goes beyond the notion of wearing whatever attribution our patients place on us. It is cognizant of the fact that we are, in fact, all things to all people, that nothing in human existence is outside our ken. "Unscrew the locks from the doors," Whitman writes in "Song of Myself" 24 (p. 41). He wants to witness all, without prejudice: "The suicide sprawls on the bloody floor of the bedroom/I witness the corpse with his dabbled hair, I note where the pistol has fallen" (p. 28). He is making here a phenomeno-logical exploration of his own consciousness, a preliminary step, Heinz Kohut (1959) would maintain a century later, to an empathic exploration of the consciousness of others.

Whitman's poetic self is capable of extraordinary tenderness and empa-thy, as we just saw in the passage about the runaway slave. At times his connection to others transcends what we normally think of as empathy. Here is another passage about slavery from "Song of Myself," in which he allows himself to completely enter into the slave's experience:

I am the hounded slave, I wince at the bite of the dogs
Hell and despair are upon me, crack and again crack the marksmen.

(p. 54)

A bit later in the same section, he writes, "I do not ask the wounded person how he feels, I myself become the wounded person" (p. 54). The ability of the artist to enter into others' lives is the gift of literature. But Whitman is not creating a character. The only character in "Song of Myself" is the author's ever-expanding, all-inclusive self. A self that is indivisible from the others that surround it.

The two famous assertions that Whitman makes in part 51 of "Song of Myself": "Do I contradict myself?/Very well then . . . I contradict myself"; and "I am large, I contain multitudes" (p. 72) can guide us toward a fully contextualized, antipositivist, dynamic systems view of the self. Whitman's self anticipates Bromberg's (1998) "multiple self states" by 150 years:

A discernible shift has been taking place with regard to psychoana-lytic understanding of the human mind and the nature of unconscious mental processes – away from the idea of a conscious/preconscious/ unconscious distinction per se, toward a view of the self as decentered, and the mind as a configuration of shifting, nonlinear, discontinuous states of consciousness in an ongoing dialectic with the healthy illusion of unitary selfhood.

(p. 3)

These nonlinear, discontinuous self-states very well may puzzle the listening analyst with their seeming contradictions, with the suddenness of their shifts, with the endless seeming variety they contain. But to Whitman, the requirement that we conform to some unitary, bounded reality is unambiguously an imposition of doubting society ("Trippers and askers surround me," p. 28) or of one's own shame and self-doubt: "Who need be afraid to merge?/Undrape . . . you are not guilty to me, nor stale nor discarded" (p. 31).

Listen to Whitman's catalog of the contexts that challenge or rebuff the free self's unfolding:

> Trippers and askers surround me,
> People I meet, the effect upon me of my early life or the ward and
>   city I live in, or the nation,
> The latest dates, discoveries, inventions, societies, authors old and
>   new,
> My dinner, dress, associates, looks, compliments, dues,
> The real or fancied indifference of some man or woman I love,
> The sickness of one of my folks or of myself, or ill-doing or loss or
>   lack of money, or depressions or exaltations,
> Battles, the horrors of fratricidal war, the fever of doubtful news, the
>   fitful events;
> These come to me days and nights and go from me again,
> But they are not the Me myself.

(p. 28)

Though at times it seems that Whitman's self merges with the environment, here it is something distinct, separate. Whitman's self, in keeping with his acceptance of contradictions, is simultaneously the whole field of existence and an experiencing entity within that field.

Whitman's relationality

Whitman's self, with its mysticism and relationality, can be seen as a precursor of current psychoanalytic thinking. Contemporary psychoanalysis, with its emphasis on a phenomenological exploration of personal experience, its privileging of the therapist's intuition and its relational contextuality, has a distinctly American lineage, from Whitman and Emerson on up through William James to Harry Stack Sullivan to Heinz Kohut and on to Stephen Mitchell and Robert Stolorow. Pragmatic, experience-near, big-hearted.

As Emerson (2003) said in his address to the Harvard Divinity School:

> whilst the doors of the temple stand open, night and day, before every man, and the oracles of this truth cease never, it is guarded by one stern condition: this namely; it is an intuition. It cannot be received at second hand. Truly speaking, it is provocation, not instruction that I can receive from another soul. What he announces, I must find true in me, or wholly reject . . .
>
> (p. 65)

Or James (1920) phenomenologically investigating the moment when the intolerable isolation of neurosis and depression overwhelms us:

> a whiff of melancholy, things that sound a knell, for fugitive as they may be, they bring a feeling of coming from a deeper region and often have an appalling convincingness. The buzz of life ceases at their touch as a piano-string stops sounding when the damper falls upon it.
>
> (p. 250)

All somehow inviting us to participate imaginatively in the life of the other as a way of fully participating in our own life. One primary, anti-Cartesian intuition: we do not live as thinking entities, knowing our existence only as a mental representation, but as vulnerable beings, our minds and hearts blown open by direct experience of the other.

And behind this tradition, Whitman:

> Oxen that rattle the yoke or halt in the shade, what is that you
>   express in your eyes?
> It seems to me more than all the print I have read in my life.
>
> (p. 35)

Whitman anticipates the tilt toward relationship in contemporary psy-choanalysis where the question "Who are you?" becomes "Who are we together?" His work, though it changed in tone, remained constant in his extraordinary capacity to show love and understanding for everything his poetic eye gazed on

> This is the press of a bashful hand . . . this is the float and odor of hair
> This is the touch of my lips to yours . . . this is the murmur of yearning.
> (p. 42)

Think Kohut (1984), extending his pinky for a lost patient to grasp. Think Stolorow, Brandchaft, and Atwood relationally reframing the border-line condition as a search for a stabilizing selfobject: "What is called the 'borderline' does not rest in a pathological condition located solely in the patient. Rather, it lies in phenomena arising in an intersubjective field, consisting of a precarious, vulnerable self in a failing, archaic selfobject bond" (1987, p. 130).

What can Whitman's sense of empathy as an imaginative merger with another add to our understanding of the contemporary psychoanalytic proj-ect? Am I, as a therapist, a tripper and asker, hammering against apparent contradictions, pursuing the patient through ruses and evasions, pursuing the disavowed, repressed truth at the core of their dilemma? Is my job to help the patient move toward liberating insights? It is a complex question. The poet in me might be ready to surrender to the flow, the image stream, the unfolding of different self-states. But where does this leave my thera-peutic self-concept as an effective change-agent who has a solution to my patients' suffering? Patients who often will not/cannot open their selves to the world, cannot play in the androgynous sensual universe that Whitman at his finest inhabits. For these patients, it is Whitman's exquisite attun-ement to suffering, to the cry of the northern goose who has lost his mate, to the fragrance of lilacs blooming in the spring of unmentionable loss that I draw on. I try to listen to the different music of hope and despair, the for-ward and the trailing edge and to have faith that out of my receptiveness, something new will emerge. "I believe," "I hear," "I am with" Whitman intones, as if by refrain. Analogously, I try to sharpen my senses to the momentary shifts, to be ready for the moment when the patient says, with quiet, shining eyes, "This hour I tell things in confidence/I might not tell everybody but I will tell you" (p. 43).

However much we conceive of psychoanalytically informed psycho-therapy as a "talking cure," it does not take place between disembodied "talking heads." Whitman's self is fully embodied, and in this, too, he can be a guide for the contemporary therapist.

Whitman and the body

One of the projects Whitman undertakes in his poetry is undoing the West-ern separation of the erotic life of the body from the spiritual life of the mind. Particularly in "I Sing the Body Electric," Whitman undermines the Christian notion of the body as a place of sin, a fallen home that the soul must dwell in. Instead he maintains, "if the body were not the soul, what is the soul?" (Whitman, 1983, p. 76). Without shame, Whitman allows himself to connect erotically with all those around him, male and female: "the play of masculine muscles through clean setting trousers and waist straps" (p. 77); or the female's "hair, bosom, hips, bend of legs, negligent falling hands" (p. 79).

Overcoming this dichotomy between psyche and soma lies at the core of the contemporary psychoanalytic project as well. As Rappoport (2015) writes, "The body self and somatic component in the analytic dyad is a crucial, albeit often underestimated, aspect of the relational field." In order for the therapist to participate fully in the patient's embodied life, he must also be present in his own body. This kind of body-to-body communica-tion lies at the very origin of human development. It underlies the famous cross-modal "little shimmy" that Daniel Stern (1985) describes the mother offering to her baby.

But wholly surrendering the clinical moment to the sexual is both obvi-ously and complexly problematic. Holding erotic longings and feelings in a potential rather than actual space allows them to move freely from the eros of infancy to the complexities of adult sexual longing. Whitman's poetic gaze, which caresses but does not grip its object, offers us a way forward here.

In his prose work *Democratic Vistas* (2010), Whitman makes a dis-tinction between "*amative*," or sexual, amorous love and the intense and loving comradeship of "*adhesive*" love. Adhesive love that adds self to self, as opposed to a love that possesses or dominates, underlies much of Whitman's erotically charged but surprisingly chaste poetry. (I am inviting my therapist-reader here to put aside the homoerotic component of this

adhesive love and look at adhesive love as that of the poet for his subject
or of the analyst for the analysand.)

> To be surrounded by beautiful, curious, breathing, laughing flesh is
>   enough,
> To pass among them or touch any one, or rest my arm ever so lightly
> round his or her neck for a moment, what is this then?
> I do not ask any more delight, I swim in it as in a sea.
>
> (Whitman, 1983, p. 78)

In order to fully participate in an embodied intersubjective relationship, the
therapist must not only attune to the body of the patient but fully inhabit
his or her own body. Here, Whitman's "I Sing the Body Electric" can be
particularly instructional. The poem's culmination, which reads like a contemporary body-scan meditation, takes the readers on a tour of their own
body, be it a "man's, woman's, child's, youth's, husband's, mother's." We
descend from "Head, neck, hair, ears" (p. 82) down through "the lung-
sponges, the stomach sac, the bowels sweet and clean," to "Ankles, instep,
foot-ball, toes, toe-joints, the heel" to "Love looks, love perturbations and
risings" (p. 83).

After some time studying Beatrice Beebe's (Beebe, Cohen, and
Lachmann, 2016) split-camera exploration of the interaction between
four-month-old infants and their mothers, I am particularly taken by
Whitman's extolling the "Poise on the hips, leaping, reclining, embracing,
arm-curving and tightening,/The continual changes of the flex of the
mouth, and around the eyes." And for the meditation-minded, "The cir-
cling rivers/the breath, and breathing it in and out." And his conclusion,
banishing the distinction between psyche and soma: "O I say now, these
are the soul!" (p. 83).

Grief and trauma

In the face of the trauma and carnage of the Civil War, including the assas-
sination of his beloved President Lincoln, the youthful exuberance of
"Song of Myself" gives way in Whitman's later work to poems of witness
and elegy. Working as a nurse for wounded soldiers in Washington during the war, Whitman was as close to carnage and suffering as you can be
without actually being a soldier. In his poem "The Wound Dresser," he

writes of walking up and down the ward with "the bandages, water and sponge/Straight and swift to my wounded I go," having left the world of "gain and appearance and mirth" (Whitman, 1983, p. 249) behind at the hospital door. Here Whitman anticipates Stolorow's (2007) conception of traumatized persons as living in a world apart, having lost their faith in the "absolutisms of daily life," the illusions that buffer us from buffeting loss.

Whitman sees that his poetic duty is to witness and document suffering, and to provide a modicum of comfort to the dying:

> The crush'd head I dress, (poor crazed hand tear not the bandage
>   away,)
> The neck of the cavalry-man with the bullet through and through I
> examine,
> Hard the breathing rattles, quite glazed already the eye, yet life
> struggles hard,
> (Come sweet death! Be persuaded O beautiful death! In mercy come
> quickly.)
>
> (Whitman, 1983, p. 250)

The parentheses bracket off his subjectivity from his actions and observations. The two together form a whole. Whitman's heartbreaking wishes are like an invisible hand that guides his actions.

In his elegy to Lincoln, "When Lilacs Last in the Dooryard Bloom'd," Whitman notes the great irony that confronts the grief-stricken. Life, with its "ever returning spring" (Whitman, 1983, p. 264), goes on, even as for the griever time has seemed to stop:

> O powerful western fallen star!
> O shades of night – O moody, tearful night!
> O great star disappear'd – O the black murk that hides the star!
> O cruel hands that hold me powerless – O helpless soul of me!
> O harsh surrounding clouds that will not free my soul

he writes, while in the very next section there's "the lilac-bush tall-growing with heart shaped leaves of rich green,/With many a pointed blossom rising delicate, with the perfume strong I love" (Whitman, 1983, p. 264). Whitman is alive to the juxtapositions – me and you, the self and nature, the present moment and memories – that form the core of grief. He carefully tracks the movement of Lincoln's cortege, noting the contrast of the living details of towns and cities, the "thousand voices rising strong and solemn," with the mute coffin.

Through his careful documentation of his own and his nation's grief, Whitman earns the mystical comfort with which he concludes the poem, where death is transformed into a kind of comforting mother, enfolding us all. In this, he (most likely unconsciously) echoes the words of the Hebrew mourner's Kaddish ("Magnified, sanctified"), which praises the miracle of life and never mentions death. He writes:

> Prais'd be the fathomless universe,
> For life and joy and for objects and knowledge curious,
> And for love, sweet love – but praise! praise! praise!
> And for the sure-enwinding arms of cool-enfolding death.
> Dark mother always gliding near with soft feet, . . .
> (Whitman, 1983, p. 269)

If one, as a reader or a practitioner, lacks the ability to welcome death's maternal comfort, one can wrap oneself instead in the comfort of Whitman's poetic vision, drawing it up like a shawl against the chill.

The trauma of loss gets personified in the call of the widower goose in "Out of the Cradle Endlessly Rocking." Whitman gives voice to the male goose who has lost his mate and sings, "uselessly, uselessly, all the night" (p. 203):

> *O Past! O happy life! O songs of joy!*
> *In the air, in the woods, over fields,*
> *Loved! Loved! Loved! Loved! Loved!*
> *But by my mate no more, no more with me!*
> *We two together no more.*
> (Whitman, 1983, p. 203;
> italics in original)

The poet takes the bird's plaintive call as an instruction, a loss of innocence that opens him to a deeper knowledge:

> Never more shall the cries of unsatisfied love be absent from me,
> Never again leave me to be the peaceful child I was before what there in the night,

By the sea under the yellow, sagging moon
The messenger there arous'd, the fire, the sweet hell within,
The unknown want, the destiny of me.

(Whitman, 1983, p. 204)

With the wounded soldiers, the grief-stricken nation, or the wild, for-lorn goose, Whitman describes grief and trauma in relational terms. This, I think, is a great gift to practitioners. Though he carefully tracks his own subjective responses to the events he witnesses, in the end, there is no separation between the grief-stricken and the poet. They form one, inter-subjective whole. The poetic act is an act of surrender to the whole range of human experience, and out of this surrender, the poet's song emerges, a third term. Here is the ending of "Out of the Cradle Endlessly Rocking," where the sea, ceaselessly whispering "Death," becomes a life-affirming muse:

My own songs awaked from that hour
And with them the key, the word up from the waves,
The word of the sweetest song of all songs
That strong delicious word which, creeping to my feet,
(Or like some old crone rocking the cradle, swathed in sweet
garments, bending aside,)
The sea whisper'd me.

(Whitman, 1983, p. 205)

Case vignette

The following vignette indicates the way Whitman's expanded sense of the self guided my understanding of a couple's interaction around their differing responses to the husband's traumatic history. There is a 15-to 20-year gap in age between Richard, a retired college teacher, and Leslie, an artist. Both have traumatic childhood histories. Richard grew up in a working-class family dominated by his father's physical and emotional abuse. Leslie's parents were wrapped up in their own lives and failed to adequately protect her or respond to her being molested by a neighbor.

The incident I am discussing happened when Leslie found a 40-year-old letter from Richard's father. In the letter, his father, facing death, asked Richard to forgive him if he had been too hard or harsh with him. Leslie was profoundly moved by the letter, which she never knew existed, and which belied the impression that Richard had given her about his father. "It is a beautiful letter. It offers you even now a chance for you to reconcile with him. He asks for forgiveness, and you should give it to him. We have to forgive if we are to move on with our lives."

It is Richard who brought up this topic in therapy. He felt violated by Leslie's reading the letter, and he felt misunderstood in her pushing him to forgive his father. "I take out this letter and read it once a year," he tells us. "Each time I have the same response. 'You narcissistic bastard. This is all about you. You want my forgiveness so you can die at peace. But what about me, what about my brother? Why couldn't you come to me directly and tell me you're sorry, instead of writing me a damn letter?'"

I was moved by both of their seemingly irreconcilable takes on the letter. And I was at first tempted to see Leslie's response as pertaining to her own history, her own wish to have gotten a letter like that from her parents that would have enabled her to move toward forgiveness. A clash of two very different subjectivities. But something gave me permission to take a more Whitmanesque approach, in which all of our histories belong to one another. Though I could understand Richard's sense of boundary violation, I didn't quite see it that way.

Surely the personal histories of our intimate partners become part of the "multitudes" our selves contain. I said to Richard, "I can certainly see how you feel that Leslie is overstepping your boundary and telling you how to feel about your father. But there might be another way to look at this. Perhaps something gets expanded when, in relationships, we live each other's lives. Perhaps Richard's implacable anger can become part of your story, as if it were yours, Leslie. And perhaps Leslie's generosity and forgiveness can become part of yours, Richard."

In retrospect, my response was guided by something Coburn (2014) calls our analytic attitude – a set of assumptions, values or organizing principles that serve to bend the analytic intersubjective system toward the emergence of a healthier, more complex organization. Of note in this regard was the way my attitude toward the couple allowed for – rather than trying to clarify – the inevitable confusions and mergers of identity that relationships bring. In the words of dynamic systems theorists Thelan and Smith (1994, p. xvi), dynamic systems are "messy, fluid and context dependent," a sentiment with which I can imagine Whitman concurring.

For Richard and Leslie, my comments and the attitude that informed them did not lead to a dramatic breakthrough. Rather, over time, my accepting of seemingly irreconcilable differences, along with my refraining from insisting that self-differentiation was the highest goal in relationship, led to a gradual softening of the edges of their conflicts. There was also a slight but noticeable increase in the comfort they could take in each other.

How much we, as therapists, can learn by Whitman's willingness to embrace seeming opposites – "Loved! Loved! Loved!" (1983, p. 203) and "Death death death death death" (p. 205) – not as dialectics leading to some greater synthesis but as part of a mystical sense of oneness. Tacking back and forth between the three subjectivities in a couples therapy session, I find myself comforted and emboldened by Whitman's guileless assertion: "Do I contradict myself?/Very well then . . . I contradict myself" (p. 72).

Chapter 10

Wallace Stevens

The world imagined

In the late fall or early winter, twilight sneaks up the walls of my office in Oakland, near Lake Merritt. The lake and the white apartment buildings on the hills behind it hold onto the light a moment before relinquishing it. A session that starts out in full light can end in outlines and shadows. Sometimes I'll be too wrapped up in what a patient is telling me – a depressed woman has decided to take up the piano again after a 15-year hiatus; a man recalls his father saying, "If we don't sleep here tonight, we'll never sleep here again," after the coroner has removed his mother's suicide-body – that it is not until the check-writing or handshake that I remember to get up and flick on the pole lamp by the couch.

"Light the first lights of evening," Wallace Stevens writes in his poem "Final Soliloquy of the Interior Paramour," "as in a room/Where we rest and for small reason think/The world imagined is the ultimate good" (Stevens, 1978, p. 524).

Our analytic imagination is the vehicle through which we participate in our patients' lives. Through it, we can hear the first tentative notes of fingers on a keyboard, see an empty room after the paramedics have removed a mother's body. Some of our patients are trapped inside their self as if it were a prison, denied the comfort of contact with the actual. Others are crushed by the weight of the world, their needs and wishes thwarted at every turn. For both, "the world imagined" is a potential third term, a path to a living connection with a vitalizing other.

Winnicott's (1971b) notion of *potential space*, the location "of play, which expands into creative living and to the whole of the cultural life of man" (p. 138), is relevant here. This potential space lies between "personal or psychic reality and the actual world." Potential space, Winnicott adds, "can be looked upon as sacred to the individual in that it is here that the individual experiences creative living." More recently, Malcom Slavin (Slavin and Kriegman, 1992) stresses the evolutionary function of art as path to the amelioration of existential dread. So we turn to a poet like Stevens to guide us, through acts of imagination, toward a leavening.

Stevens is a poet of the imagination. For him, it is the one transcendent good. Through the imagination, his poetry is able to span many contradictions – between a vivid sensuality and a formal reserve, between faith and disbelief, between an idealism-based philosophical bent and the myriad of details like the "roller of big cigars." A serious, philosophical poet, Stevens can at times also be quite funny as he describes a funky world in which "The only emperor is the emperor of ice cream" (1978, p. 64). Stevens, like many of our patients, at times seems quite sad and lonely, haunted by both "Nothing that is not there and the nothing that is" ("The Snowman," 1978, p. 9). But like his protagonist in "The Idea of Order at Key West," he is also, in his solitude, the creator of his own world, "the single artificer of the world/In which she sang" (1978, p. 128).

Wallace Stevens (1879–1955) was born in Reading, Pennsylvania. He was educated at Harvard, completed law school in 1903, and spent the majority of his career working as a surety bond attorney for the Hartford Insurance Company. He eventually became a vice president of that company. (It is worth noting that the three great American poets of his generation, Stevens, William Carlos Williams and T.S. Eliot, all had successful, nonpoetic careers.) He married a woman from Reading and stayed with her the rest of his life, though it was reputed to be an unhappy marriage. A late bloomer, Stevens published his first book, *Harmonium*, at age 44. Only in his annual trips to Key West does Stevens's biography reflect anything to match the sensuous world one finds in his poems, which also have a philosophical bent and occasionally veer toward the surreal.

Poetry for Stevens is, like psychoanalysis, a secular religion. Here the poor in spirit, the pure of heart, as well as the impure in spirit and those trapped in the material world, can come and find solace under "a single shawl/Wrapped tightly around us, since we are poor." This from his magnificent late poem, "The Final Soliloquy of the Interior Paramour" (1978, p. 524), which we will be examining in some detail. His elegiac late poems like the "Final Soliloquy" live between a late flicker of light and oncoming darkness. Unifying this contradiction between light and dark, between belief and skepticism, is Stevens's faith in the redemptive power of the imagination, his conviction that the mind is shapely, capable of creating "a whole, an order": "After one has abandoned a belief in god, poetry is that essence which takes its place as life's redemption" he writes in "Adagia" (1982, p. 158).

In order to understand the redemptive nature of imagination, we must first understand the unredeemed materiality it is pitched against. "The World is too much with us," writes Wordsworth (2004, p. 144). The depressed feel hemmed in by materiality. "Heavenly hurt it gives us," writes Emily Dickinson (1960, p. 118). In a psychic state of depression, the deadness of things reminds us of the deadness inside. Conversely, when, through our imagination, the world becomes animated (or – given our exile from the child's imaginary world – reanimated), it vitalizes us.

In his book on Stevens, *Things Merely Are*, the philosopher and critic Simon Critchley (2005) writes,

> common reality can press in on the self, the city becomes oppressive and the self depressive. The world becomes a deafening, violent place, dominating by an ever-enlarging incoherence of information and the constant presence of war.
>
> (p. 10)

By contrast, he continues,

> The poetic act, the act of the mind, illuminates the surface of things with imagination's beam. . . . Through it we detect what we might call *the movement of the self* in those things, plate, bread, wine, water, rock, tree, moon.
>
> (p. 10)

It is the provision of this "movement of self" – as opposed to a self that cannot move at all – that links the imagination to the therapy process.

Heinz Kohut (1971) spoke of the "mirror transference," a wish for the patient to have their world reflected back to them. But in fact a mirror is deadeningly literal. It is only through our imagination that we can participate in a patient's inner life. In an example we will turn to shortly, a patient who lost his leg to cancer as an adolescent has told the story many times. But something lifted and transformed when he was able to convey to our collective imagination what he had been through.

In Stevens's work, the richness of his poetic imagination provides solace and compensation for loss – the loss of religion as an organizer of the world, the loss of received authority and the lack of intimacy with his controlling and reserved wife. But shining through this elegiac tone is the beauty of his language, his sensual appreciation of the world. Celebration married to elegy.

The intensest rendezvous

By way of examining what Stevens's view of the redemptive power of the imagination might offer therapists, let us turn to a consideration of "The Final Soliloquy of the Interior Paramour" (1978, p. 524). It is one of the last poems Stevens published in his lifetime. Its notes of deep resolution and its consoling voice have been a sustaining force for me since I first encountered it a number of years ago. Here is the poem in its entirety:

Final Soliloquy of the Interior Paramour

Light the first light of evening, as in a room
In which we rest and, for small reason, think
The world imagined is the ultimate good.

This is, therefore, the intensest rendezvous.
It is in that thought that we collect ourselves,
Out of all the indifferences, into one thing:

Within a single thing, a single shawl
Wrapped tightly round us, since we are poor, a warmth,
A light, a power, the miraculous influence.

Here, now, we forget each other and ourselves.
We feel the obscurity of an order, a whole,
A knowledge, that which arranged the rendezvous.

Within its vital boundary, in the mind.
We say God and the imagination are one . . .
How high that highest candle lights the dark.

Out of this same light, out of the central mind,
We make a dwelling in the evening air,
In which being there together is enough.

Rereading it here, I recall my first encounter. Black Oak Books in Berkeley, now gone from its North Berkeley location, was the home of some of the most wonderful poetry readings I ever attended. Each year for the holidays, they printed a beautiful broadside of a poem. "The Final Soliloquy of the Interior Paramour" was one. I had it framed, and for many years it hung in my "inner sanctum" – a converted walk-in closet in my office where I kept my filing cabinets and answering machine. Its presence would console me between patients.

It is a love poem, a poem of reconciliation between the poet and his beloved, written toward the end of their life together. Like all such poems, it is also part elegy. "When I heard you were dead Heraclitus/tears came, and I remembered how often/you and I had talked the sun to bed," writes the third-century BCE poet Callimachus, as translated by Edmund Keeley (Constantine et al., 2010, p. 238). "Be patient that I address you in a poem,/ there is no other/fit medium," writes Stevens's contemporary William Carlos Williams in his late poem "To Daphne and Virginia" (1962, p. 246).

But here, the aging lovers are interior characters, soul and self, anima and animus, two of what Bromberg (1998) calls "a multiplicity of selves." Stevens has used his imagination to figure the interior workings of his own mind. The intrapsychic becomes exquisitely interpersonal. Perhaps a bit of biography will make this achievement even more significant: As the noted Stevens critic Helen Vandler (1986) points out, any tender or passionate poetry Stevens wrote stands in sharp contrast to his own family life. Stevens had a disastrous marriage to a woman their daughter described as suffering from mental illness; his disapproving parents didn't attend the wedding, and he remained permanently estranged from them thereafter. In this context, his rendezvous with the interior paramour, his inner lover, gains poignancy. Given the title's indication that it is the inner lover who is the speaker of the poem, the poet himself becomes the recipient of her warmth and consolation – an experience in his art that was sadly lacking in his life. The poem is alchemical in nature; it achieves the alchemist's goal of fusing opposites. The alchemical wedding takes place under a shawl/canopy. The marriage of self and soul create not external but internal gold. Or at least the golden glow of a pair of lovers bathed in candlelight.

In order for me to describe what moves me in this poem, I need to state what I find it standing against. The poem is an assertion of meaning in the face of "nothing that is not there" – the void of nonexistence – "and the nothing that is": the existential disconnection and emptiness we feel when we confront that void ("The Snowman," Stevens, 1978, p. 9). Against this combination of nothings, the poem asserts the possibility of a some-thing, a world imagined. A world where the divisions between our mind and the world outside of our mind, and between the different selves inside us, can be unified. It is precisely these types of divisions that our patients come to therapy to heal.

The internal paramour whose soliloquy this poem speaks is aligned with Jung's notion of the soul or anima. For men, it is a feminine aspect of the self. It is also an example of what Bollas (1987) refers to as "the self as object," "an intersubjective relation to the self" through which "we can analyse how a person holds and relates to himself" (p. 42). At this late hour, the speaker of this poem relates to the self with great tenderness and reconciliation. It is a talisman of healing, of possibility for integration. It speaks to analytic possibility.

The particular occasion of the poem is a moment of deep connection as evening, both literally and figuratively, comes on. An exquisitely inter-subjective moment between two internal characters: the self and its imag-ined "other." It is not grand in nature. For some "small reason" the lover's delight as they alight on a moment of commonly held philosophical truth: "The world imagined is the ultimate good." That there is good to be had at all in our postmodern, relativistic world, let alone *ultimate* good, seems ground for celebration. With understated eloquence, the word "ultimate" announces a profoundly spiritual poem.

One notices from the first the stateliness of the triadic stanza form. There is a deep and satisfying beauty here; it sits on the page, as well as in the air of our hearing, in a profound equipoise. In concert with the triplet stanzas of the poem, we note that there are really three terms in this poem: the poet, his "interior paramour," and the world they perceive (or in Stevens's term, "imagine") around them. As with the Holy Trinity, the three are one – collected by the imagination into "one thing" into which, like poor, holy pilgrims, the poet and his paramour/soul are gathered.

The emergence of this in-gathering oneness leads me to associate to the psychoanalytic notion of "the third" (Ogden, 2004) – the other, the greater than – that emerges from a dyadic encounter. I read this poem as saying that the third is the "world imagined," which, in turn, "imagines" or envelops us: "a light, a power, the miraculous influence." We do from time to time find ourselves and our patients enveloped with this mysterious influence. Because we are poor in such moments, we must use few words, or none at all.

"That which arranged the rendezvous" is not the poet, not the therapist, but something greater, something divine. Together we feel "the obscurity of an order," "within its vital boundary, in the mind." All poetry, my great teacher Denise Levertov maintained, is, by virtue of its very existence, spiritual poetry. "God and the imagination are one."

"How high the moon?" asked Les Paul and Mary Ford's version of the standard, on the charts for 25 weeks in 1951, close to this poem's composition. "How high the highest candle lights the dark," writes Stevens. It is both an exclamation and a question. However high the candle penetrates, the dark remains, outside, around us. The poem is about love not metaphysics. In his poem "The Idea of Order at Key West" (1978, pp. 128–130), the female figure is a mystery, a solitude, a singer who becomes through her singing "the single artificer of the world." "There never was a world for her/Except the one she singing made," the poet observes. But here the poet and his paramour have made a world "out of the central mind," which is both the mind of the imagination and the mind of god. It is not in the soaring of the highest light, but here, in the arms of each other, the lover, the consoling mother, returns. "We make a dwelling in the evening air/In which being there together is enough."

Case vignette: the color of the chemo

The following case vignette illustrates the power of imagination in creating a moment of intersubjective conjunction, and the power of that conjunction, in turn, to help resolve the tension between two competing internal realities, one of an ostensibly happy daily life and the other of trauma and alienation.

Aaron is a middle-aged academic and artist who survived two childhood traumas: growing up with a mentally ill and abusive father and suffering bone cancer as an adolescent. The disease eventually resulted in the amputation of his leg at the knee. Our early work focused on the trauma of witnessing the father's angry and occasionally violent outbursts directed most often at his younger sister, who ended up severely mentally ill. The trauma of his amputation, and equally, the trauma of his agonizing years of treatment "while other kids were thinking about girls and sports," were slower to emerge.

Though Aaron had told the story of his illness, with its endless-seeming surgeries and treatments, something about this second trauma remained elusive for quite some time. On one occasion, though, Aaron, describing the horror of chemotherapy (which in those days was given at full strength, and repeatedly), remembered a vivid detail. He recalled walking in the hospital past the stations where the other children, some quite young, were receiving their treatments. He told of the vivid, unearthly-colored chemo agents in their I.V. bottles, synthetic shades of red and green and yellow. And of how, after his treatment, his vomit would have the same unearthly color as the chemo agent.

These vivid visual details engaged not only my empathy, as I felt what his pain and terror must have been like, but also my imagination. The colors of the chemo agents seemed to take on a kind of primal force in my mind's eye. We recall Robert Hass's notion of images as "closer to pure story" (1984, p. 275). The abstract notion of Aaron's cancer treatment, which stretched on for many years, became encapsulated in the picture of those unearthly colors and the children waiting to receive them. And of vomit in the gutter, beneath the taxi door. However different in valence from the shawl and the candle in the Stevens poem, the image of the chemo colors shared their ability to create a third that organizes – or reorganizes – the world between two people.

As our work progressed, the images became a way for us to point to our collective understanding of his trauma. One or the other of us would only have to say "it was like all those colorful chemo agents" to invoke our mutually held understanding. And the image helped contextualize Aaron's independent decision to end his ordeal after three years of medical treatment and undergo amputation so he could stop being one of the children lined up with their different-colored chemo agents.

The particular session I wish to describe here took place in the fourth year of therapy, approximately one year after the death of his mother, who had long endured a crippling neurological disease. His mother courageously opted for what amounted to a legalized euthanasia, for which Aaron was present. After the initial grief, Aaron descended into a depressive mourning period in which his work and even his considerable successes lost all color. He often felt like an imposter as he lectured or saw his work displayed in galleries.

In the session under consideration, he is describing having had to euthanize a beloved cat over the weekend. It was extremely difficult for him to watch, but he forced himself to look as the vet administered the "light-purple" euthanizing agent. It took just a quick mutual gaze for us to invoke our shared imaginative understanding of the agent's colors. As if seamlessly adding words to our heretofore silent conversation, Aaron added, "of course there were no chemo agents exactly that color."

Then, under the influence of this emergent third, Aaron had the following association. "Later that day, I was sitting in the backyard, where we have a propane outdoor heater. I thought that propane could explode at any moment. Then I looked at the glass table, and I thought that table could shatter at any moment, and the shards would be cutting me" (an image he later in the session associated to the endless rounds of scarring surgeries he endured). And then he said, "That's the way I live, David, always going from one terror to the next."

This insight amounted to a moment of mentalization, of looking at and acknowledging the contribution of his own mind to his lived reality. As Fonagy et al. (2002) and his colleagues have pointed out, the capacity for mentalization is an emergent property of the dyadic caregiver/child system. Once in place, it liberates the child (and, by extension, the patient) from the rule of psychic equivalence – if I feel it, it must be true. Under the collective shawl of our shared imagination, Aaron was able to look at his posttraumatic sensorium as a mental product, not an omnipresent reality. In the weeks following this session, he reported moments of greater calm. His sense of being an imposter at work lessened, and he reported that his academic work, though still alienating, had at least become bearable.

Through an act of our imagination, the vials of chemo agents had been transformed into something speakable. They became an image, like the shawl and candle in the Stevens poem. As in the Stevens poem, the distinction between the inter- and the intra-subjective blurs. On the one hand, this session about the euthanasia referenced and replayed a previous "moment of meeting" (Boston Change Process Group, 2010) between therapist and patient over the image of the chemo agents. At the same time, it marked a profound meeting between two internal characters: Aaron's artistic self, able to vividly describe the power of exploding tanks and cutting shards, and the traumatized child, reeling from moment after moment of incomprehensible medical and familial horror. It was tempting to interpret the images of exploding tanks and cutting shards as related to his twin traumas of father and cancer, but I forbore, realizing that we had come to a moment "in which being there together is enough."

Chapter 11

William Carlos Williams

How to look, how to listen

Heinz Kohut's (1971, 1977) advocacy for an "experience-near" psychoanalytic listening stance has an ally in the poetry of William Carlos Williams. Kohut urged us to abandon our theory-based preconceptions and empathically immerse ourselves in our patient's immediate experience. He wasn't advocating, as some have maintained, an abandonment of the depth in depth psychology. Tuning in to the patient's immediate, moment-to-moment experience reveals the entryway to those depths. Here is Williams, describing the loneliness and ecstasy of a moment in a busy husband's life:

Danse Russe

If I when my wife is sleeping
and the baby and Kathleen
are sleeping
and the sun is a flame-white disc
in silken mists
above shining trees, –
if I in my north room
dance naked, grotesquely
before my mirror
waving my shirt round my head
and singing softly to myself:
"I am lonely, lonely.
I was born to be lonely,
I am best so!"

> If I admire my arms, my face,
> my shoulders, flanks, buttocks
> against the yellow drawn shades, –
> Who shall say I am not
> the happy genius of my household?
> (Williams, 1991a, p. 86)

This is an example of what Kohut would call healthy narcissism and grandiosity, yoked to the creative expression of a shirt-waving dance in front of the mirror. Notice the details: the "flame-white disc" of the sun shining through the silken mist, the silhouette of his buttocks "against the yellow drawn shades." Notice too the intimacy he provides for the reader, naming his older daughter, describing a peaceful moment in a perhaps turbulent household. Williams's "happy genius" is, of course, his poetic genius. But it is also genius in its alternate meaning of identity or spirit. This is the genius of everyman, trapped in life and seeking a moment's transcendence. It is only in the particulars that this genius can be known. Our consultant, Dr. Williams, taking time off from his pediatric practice, tells us that everything important about our patients can be found in the details we mine through empathic listening and careful observation.

Williams's famous statement from his long poem *Paterson*, "No ideas but in things," could be the slogan of an experience-near psychoanalysis. But his project is not merely to listen and observe closely. It was to reveal the universal themes found in his immediate experience. Here's the complete quote:

> – Say it, no ideas but in things –
> nothing but the blank faces of the houses
> and cylindrical trees
> bent, forked by preconception and accident –
> split, furrowed, creased, mottled, stained –
> secret – into the body of the light!
> (1963, pp. 14–15)

So it is not only the language of things he is after but also the ideas that emerge at the boundary between perception and the thing perceived.

A couple of clinical examples: (1) A woman whose war-traumatized mother told her "don't embarrass me with your emotions" found as an adult an emotional outlet in gardening. Her husband, trying to be helpful, bought the wrong brand of fir mulch and spread it. "But it's the wrong color," she wanted to exclaim. Then, catching herself, she said instead, "Oh well, it will weather and change color with time." (2) "I never resent taking care of her," said a man whose wife was slowly succumbing to Alzheimer's. "It's just that sometimes I feel with her that I am talking into my pillow." The ear picks up the note of newfound resilience, the note of devotion mixed with grief.

Overview

William Carlos Williams (1883–1963) was a pediatrician and family doctor. He maintained a practice in Rutherford, New Jersey, throughout his adult life, writing poetry in what little spare time he had. Famously, he had a rolltop desk in his consulting room that he would open up to write between patients. He says in his *Autobiography*: "My 'medicine' was the thing which gained me access to these secret gardens of the self. It lay there, another world, in the self. I was permitted by my medical badge to follow the poor, defeated body into those gulfs and grottos" (Williams, 1967, quoted in Wagner, 1976, p. x).

A few examples:

> Her milk don't seem to . . .
> She's always hungry but . . .
> She seems to gain all right,
> I don't know.
> > ("Detail," 1991b,
> > pp. 14–15)

> Whyn't you bring me
> A good letter? One with
> Lots of money in it.
> I could make use of that.
> Atta Boy! Atta boy!
> > ("To Greet a Letter
> > Carrier," 1991a, p. 458)

Or this, from "The Last Words of My English Grandmother":

> Oh, oh oh! She cried
> as the ambulance men lifted
> her to the stretcher –
> is this what you call
> making me comfortable?
>   (1991a, p. 465)

Speech rhythms

Dante's great innovation was to abandon Latin and write poems in his vernacular Italian. Williams's project, like Whitman's before him, involved abandoning the prosody of English poetry to find an American idiom. He was dismayed about his contemporaries Ezra Pound and T.S. Eliot abandoning America (and, by extension, American language) for Europe. Like Blake before him, he wanted to build his poetic city not on the hill of classicism but right here in his native land, be it London or Rutherford. It was for this reason that his immediate contemporary Wallace Stevens called him (to Williams's dismay) a Romantic, noting Williams's insistence that his personal experience yield universal insight. The "common language" (1963, p. 15) Williams searched for was the language he heard, the language he spoke. The universal themes it expressed were not a matter of high rhetoric but of the stops and starts, the heartbreaking pauses and quick insistencies of spoken language. Of his poetic process, he wrote, "Its movement is intrinsic, undulant, a physical more than a literary character. In a poem this movement is distinguished . . . by the character of the speech from which it arises" (quoted in Wegner, 1976, p. xiv).

The physicality Williams saw in speech dovetails nicely with modern theories of implicit and nonverbal aspects of communication: "O Tongue/licking/the sore on/her netherlip//O toppled belly," he writes in a section of his poem "Spring and All" (1991a, p. 215). And then,

> I can't die
> – moaned the old
> jaundiced woman
> rolling her
> saffron eyeballs

I can't die
I can't die.

The line breaks mark the progress of our empathic heartbreak, pausing in the enjambed sentence for a descent into our own sorrow/compassion. We pause between "old" and "jaundiced," between "her" and "saffron." Williams here has invented not just a modern poetic form but a way of notating his experience and, by extension, ours. The tongue on lip, the belly, the "I can't die." This is the way we must listen, Williams is saying. And this is the way, Williams tells us, we must listen with all our senses to our patients.

The physicality of perception

Denise Levertov (1973), in her essay "Williams and the Duende," cites this passage in Williams as exemplifying his "Franciscan sense of wonder that illumines what is accounted ordinary" (p. 257):

I never tire of the mystery
of these streets: the three baskets
of dried flowers in the high

barroom window, the gulls wheeling
above the factory, the dirty
snow – the humility of the snow
that silvers everything and is

trampled and lined with use . . .
            (1991b, pp. 108–109, quoted
                        in Levertov, 1973)

Again, the line breaks track and instruct our perception: high//barroom window, the gulls wheeling/above the factory, dirty/snow. They question our preconceptions and demand that we participate, moment by moment, with the poet's act of perception of the world around him.

You always say you want
to talk, but all the way
to Palo Alto: your seat
back, your headphones on.

– I thought
I'd let you have
some quiet.

might be a Williamsesque way of notating a couple's interaction in my
office. We "see" with our breathing, with the twitch of our muscles. With
the bolloxed crossed messages of slouching and wishing goodwill. With
the little shudder of *ouch* our patients make. With the hand at our neck, as
if protecting from a predator attack.

In his poem "By the Road to the Contagious Hospital" from his early
masterwork "Spring and All," Williams notes the resilience of life, in the
form of a weedy plant, "the stiff curl of wildcarrot leaf" next to an edifice of infirmity (1991a, p. 183). A smile that is half grimace. A young
woman's arm-sweeping gesture to convey how she felt pushed aside by
her preoccupied parents.

A journey to love

Williams's late poems explode with feeling, especially with love for his
wife Flossie. Unsentimental love:

Romance has no part in it.
The business of love is
cruelty which,
by our wills,
we transform
to live together.
            ("The Ivy Crown,"
        1991b, pp. 287–290)

The transformation of cruelty – by which I think he means the daily
slights and disappointments that make up adult relationships – into the
fabric of our ongoing life is the prime task of intimate partners. The
realization that love is a thing we make with our wills rather than an
offering of grace is hard for many couples to reconcile. To build a relationship with our will is directly opposite to finding the consolation of
a mother, and the realization brings a kind of loss, a kind of mourning.
But it is this sharing of grief which gives married love its meaning and
its durability.

"The Ivy Crown" begins:

> The whole process is a lie,
> unless
> crowned by excess
> it break forcefully
> one way or another,
> from its confinement –
> or find a deeper well.
>> (1991b, pp. 287–288)

The wish to break from the confinement of a stuck relationship or to find a deeper well for it to draw from could summarize the wants of a majority of couples, at least the ones that seek therapy. "Asphodel, That Greeny Flower" is an almost 30-page-long poem of recollection and mature love. The poem opens up to include all of literary and human history up through recent events like the atomic bomb and the execution of the Rosenbergs (1991b, p. 311).

Echoing "The Ivy Crown," the poem joins the celebratory with the mordant: "We lived long together/a life filled,/if you will/with flowers. So that/I was cheered/when I came first to know/that there were flowers also,/in hell." Love poems of the long-married are rare indeed. We recall that Dante had a wife and children, but they didn't compare for poetic and spiritual inspiration to Beatrice, whom he saw just a handful of times. "Asphodel" touches on Homer, Cezanne, Columbus's voyage and the atomic bomb but at the end returns to a recollection of his long-ago wedding:

> So moved by your presence
> a girl so pale
> and ready to faint
> that I pitied
> and wanted to protect you.
> As I think of it now,
> after a lifetime,
> it is as if
> a sweet scented flower
> were poised
> and for me did open.
>> (1991b, p. 336)

Paterson: the self as a city

Paterson (1963), Williams's late, great epic poem about Paterson, New Jersey (next door to his native Rutherford), is of particular interest to therapists for the way it depicts the self as including the wider environment and even the historical record. Williams writes "that a man in himself is a city, beginning, seeking, achieving and concluding his life in ways which the various aspects of a city may embody" (1963, author's note). Paterson the city becomes Dr. Paterson, the man, a kind of mythic hero. Whereas Whitman achieved this effect with long lists, Williams collages together sources such as old letters, newspaper clippings, well-soundings and numerous separate observations.

Other echoes of Whitman abound, especially in the accretion of observed details of American life. But where Whitman sings of the unity of all things, Williams sings of their brokenness. "Divorce is/ the sign of knowledge in our time/divorce! Divorce!" (1963, p. 28). Robert Lowell, in a jacket quote from the paperback edition, writes: "*Paterson* is Whitman's America, grown pathetic and tragic" (1963, front matter). But there is, alongside this elegiac tone, a lot of Whitman the great unifier in *Paterson:* "rolling up out of chaos/a nine months' wonder, the city/the man/, an identity" (p. 12). And, a few lines later: "the drunk, the sober; the illustrious/the gross; one." This is Whitman's self, fast-forwarded 100 years. But the project remains intact: healing. And in Williams, as in Blake, as in Stevens, this healing comes through the lifting of the world around him, via the poetic imagination, into art.

"And so to man,//to Paterson," Williams writes at the end of the Preface to Book I (1963, p. 13). Written between 1948 and 1963, *Paterson*, at least at first glance, continues the search for coherence amidst chaos that marks the Modernist project.

"What common language to unravel?" (p. 15) he asks at the beginning of his epic poem. But is unity, including the unity of the self, an illusion, a holdover of the Enlightenment: "Go to the river for/an answer/for relief from 'meaning'" (p. 135). Later, there are passages describing a tornado and a whole section devoted to a fire in the library. Perhaps, Williams seems to be saying, coherence and meaning elude us. If so, he will, like a contemporary analyst, note the different parts and the way they interact.

Including a part that will always be longing for a common language to emerge.

> Who is it spoke of April? Some
> insane engineer. There is no recurrence.
> The past is dead . . .

(p. 169)

Even then, Williams will not turn cynic. Nor will he turn to metaphysics for consolation. Instead, the doctor/poet will listen and look, will note what he sees, staying as close as he can to the matter at hand. A stance of witness and, ultimately, of love.

> And the guys from Paterson
> beat up
> the guys from Newark and told
> them to stay the hell out
> of their territory and then
> socked you one
> across the nose
> Beautiful Thing
> for good luck and emphasis
> cracking it
> till I must believe that all
> desired women have had each
> in the end
> a busted nose

(1963, p. 439)

Case vignette

> It is difficult
> to get the news from poems
> yet men die miserably every day
> for lack
> of what is found there.

(Williams, 1963, p. 318)

It would be an exaggeration to say that either Will or Gem (Gemia), a long-married couple in their early 70s, were about to die miserably for lack of something poetic in their marriage. But a poetic moment of vivid connection for each with the childhood memories of the other provided an antidote to their chronic unhappiness.

Will and Gem have been married for 35 years. Both are retired professionals, though Will continues to pursue his inventions. Gem pursues her love of cooking and the arts and, when her legs don't fail her, taking ballet classes. They are well off, go to concerts and operas and travel frequently. They are also frequently unhappy. Will grew up in the Midwest, one of five children. Gem was born in East Asia, but dislocations from World War II and its aftermath shifted her family many times before they landed in California when she was eight. Her father was often absent in her early childhood.

Gem complains of feeling lonely and unmet. Will is so often on his smart phone, tweeting his economic and political analysis, that we negotiated a "no tweeting in bed" rule. Gem repeatedly gets stuck on some unsatisfactory response Will gives to her problems, and she'll criticize it for weeks and months; Will seems genuinely perplexed and will try, somewhat analytically, to defend himself. Behind this dynamic lies a formative moment: when they first got together, Gem left another relationship, and the East Coast, to be with Will. If only Will could have helped her through her grief over the old boyfriend! Or at least left her alone to grieve. Sometimes she feels she made a big mistake. Work with Will (quite slow) involves helping him identify that, beneath his deer-in-the-headlights look of bewilderment in the face of Gem's criticism, is a world of hurt and anger. Will has been in long-term individual therapy; Gem started therapy during our treatment.

Their relationship is a "chase and dodge" sequence (Beebe and Lachmann, 2002) that has been going on for 35 years. One time Gem said the only reason she seeks to go to so many cultural events together is desperation to find some liveliness in Will. One suggestion I give them is to stop and look into each other's eyes. Recently, thinking they don't really know each other after all these years, I decided to try administering the Adult Attachment Inventory protocol (George, Kaplan, and Main, 1985). For example, "I'd like you to try to describe your relationship with your parents as a young child, if you could start from as far back as you can remember?"

Gem remembered feeling terrified to be left off at school when she started kindergarten. "But I kept myself from crying while my mother dropped me off. Once inside, I would fall apart and cry and cry while the nuns comforted me." This recollection, of a child protecting her mother from her own tears, caught Will's attention, as did a subsequent recollection. "I must have been about eight," Gem recalled. "I had never seen my mother so much as smile, but one time, through a doorway, I saw her gossiping and laughing with a group of her friends. So she is capable of liveliness!" Gem thought bitterly.

Will could summon very few early memories, almost none of his mother, whom he described as a stern and overwhelmed woman. One that caught Gem's attention was a story from when Will was about age three. "We lived near the campus where my father taught. But to get there, you had to cross Highway 91, which in those days was a two-lane road. Apparently I wandered off by myself, crossed the highway and made it to my father's office. He simply took me home and went back to work." Gem and I thought the story carried a sense of loneliness and perhaps neglect as well, but Will couldn't view it that way.

Both Will and Gem could see their present-day partners, a lifetime later, in these childhood stories with their vividly recalled details. A three-year-old showing up at his father's office. A glimpse of a mother chatting and laughing. They became a part of our shorthand vocabulary and helped the couple replace judgment with empathy. We could say to Gem, looking at Will busy with his Twitter account, there it is with your mother and her friends, all over again. Or when Gem is troubled by Will's seeming unresponsiveness to a family tragedy: "He was taught to be like that." And she would show compassion for the disavowed loneliness that would lead a three-year-old to cross a busy highway to seek out his father. Fulfillments of Williams's dictum, "no ideas but in things." The poetic details Williams found in things and brought to the page were the difference between life and a kind of death in life. The famous passage about getting the news from poems with which we began this vignette concludes (1963, p. 318):

Hear me out
for I too am concerned
and every man
who wants to die at peace in his bed
besides.

Chapter 12

Deconstructing racism
Claudia Rankine's *Citizen*

The mistake we make in our psychotherapy community is ubiquitous. Our patients are implicitly white people. Their troubles are intrapsychic or relational, not societal. Even when we have a case example of a person of color, we fail to see the cumulative effects of racism on the psyche. If they bleed, it is from family trauma, not from the death-by-a-thousand-microaggressions they suffer from overt and implicit racism. Fortunately, we have a corrective for our blindness at hand in the form of Claudia Rankine's (2014) *Citizen*, her award-winning, formally experimental long poem that explores the threads of overt and covert racism that are woven into the very fabric of American life.

Rankine offers, in media res, bits of conversations and experiences that drip with racism. Here's an example:

> Despite the fact that you have the same sabbatical schedule as everyone else, he says you are always on sabbatical. You are friends so you respond, *easy.*
> What do you mean?
> Exactly what do you mean?

> (p. 47)

By the time we have arrived at this passage, having gone through iteration after iteration of subtle and not-so-subtle racism, we know what the friend means: you are lazy, you game the system. Racist judgments that for the first speaker, identified as a friend, may be implicit. But Rankine's powerful poem, collaging as it does examples of these micro and not-so-microaggressions, situates her subjectivity squarely in the context of this kind of racism. This experience of racism is not abstract, it is embodied. As Ta-Nehisi Coates (2015) writes:

> all our phrasing – race relations, racial chasm, racial justice, racial profiling, white privilege, even white supremacy – serves to obscure that racism is a visceral experience, that it dislodges brains, blocks airways, rips muscle, extracts organs, cracks bones, breaks teeth.

(p. 10)

By accrual of incident after incident, Rankine's work documents two dimensions of racism: its ubiquitous presence in blatant and subtle ways in our society and the internal toll it takes. As an example of the latter, let us take this incident, reported near the beginning of the book. A fellow faculty member tells Rankine as they drive somewhere together that he is being forced to hire a person of color, "when there are so many great writers out there" (p. 10). Then:

> Why do you feel comfortable saying this to me? You wish the light would turn red or a police siren would go off so you could slam on the breaks, slam into the car ahead of you, fly forward so quickly that both of your faces would suddenly be exposed to the wind.

A fantasized aggression in the face of yet one more microaggression, one more betrayal from a white person whom she has befriended. And yet there is more here than a fantasy of slamming her friend's head through the windshield. It is also an aggression against the self, since both driver and passenger would be affected. And it is a plea for air, for an escape from the terrible enclosure of being trapped in a racist society. Even as racism makes her an object, Rankine documents and thereby reclaims her complex subjectivity. An act of poetic self-invention we witness in Dante, in Dickinson and Stevens, even in the self-effacement of Celan.

Rankine was born in 1963 in Kingston, Jamaica, but educated in the U.S. Her most significant work before *Citizen* was *Don't Let Me Be Lonely* (2004). She is a poet, essayist and playwright. She has held, most recently, teaching positions at Pomona College and the University of Southern California.

The self

In many ways, *Citizen* carries on the particularly American project of expanding and reconceptualizing the self we saw in Whitman, who contained multitudes, and on through Williams, who in *Paterson* used a personified city as his alter ego/protagonist. Kohut's (1971, 1977) concept of a selfobject incorporates this kind of expansion in psychoanalysis, as the other, the object, is experienced as *part* of the self, adding to its stability and aliveness. We see this poetic project carried on in Rankine, who collages a variety of materials – prose narratives, lyric passages, essays, visual arts and journalistic inquiries – into a lyric whole. Along with their stylistic diversity, the voices she incorporates display many different tones: analytical and feeling, angry and perplexed, subdued and outraged. The poet's self is the sum of these voices and found materials. The poem is subtitled "An American Lyric," tipping us that this, for all its largeness, is a personal poem, a poem about the self.

The self that Rankine offers us is one that is expanded to include the African American experience. Rankine's self includes her love for black artists and filmmakers. It is expanded as well through its connection to admired others, like the tennis star Serena Williams or the French soccer star Zinedine Zidane. But it is also a self that the world penetrates. It is a self that is permeated by the racist world it inhabits, crushed, unnamed, confused. "What do you mean?" is a constant refrain. "What exactly do you mean?" Rankine writes:

> A friend argues that Americans battle between the "historical self" and the "self self" . . . you mostly interact as friends with mutual interest and, for the most part compatible personalities; however, sometimes your historical selves, her white self and your black self, or your white self and her black self arrive with the full force of your American positioning.
>
> (p. 10)

It is as a document of the "battle" between the "self self" and the "historical self" that *Citizen* is particularly illuminating to psychoanalysis, especially since the "historical self" has been so often absent from our discourse. The very title, *Citizen*, is meant to (however ironically) address the tension between these two selves as they attempt to function in contemporary America.

A confusion of pronouns

The interplay between the historic self and the self self is but one of the shifts that *Citizen* marks with a confusion of pronouns. In the example we just looked at, "your black self, her white self" alternates with "her black self, your white self." Not only are racial identities seemingly traded here but pronouns as well. *Citizen* marks shifts between self and other, between self and self with concomitant shifts between first, second and third persons. In the example we cited at the beginning of the chapter:

> Despite the fact that you have the same sabbatical schedule as everyone else, he says you are always on sabbatical. You are friends so you respond, *easy*.
> What do you mean?
> Exactly what do you mean?

The you that has the same sabbatical schedule as everyone else is self-referential, but her friend uses "you" as the object of his judgment: "you are always on sabbatical." Now a third you, the plural, the collective enters, agentic though shaken trying to hold the connection by saying *easy*. (As if it were!) And then a direct address, what do you – person, friend? – mean. And then the awful word "exactly" changes the last you into something else entirely. Is she accusing the accuser or opening up an almost rhetorical question directed outward, to the second person plural, to society in general? Six different *you's* in three lines. You as subject, you as other, you as accuser, you as the connection, you as the accused, plural you as the accusing world. The intersubjective field between her and her friend is one in which things change shape and tone in an instant. It reminds us how race can be a gulf one moment, a conduit for communication – my black self, your black self – the next. The case vignette at the end of this chapter will show that this confusion of identities can happen in a therapeutic dyad where the patient and therapist are of different races.

"Why even speak of 'I' he dreams which/interests me almost not at all," William Carlos Williams writes in *Paterson* (1963, p. 30). But perhaps this disinterest is a form of white privilege. Rankine rarely uses the pronoun "I," but she does return constantly to the lyric "you," the pronoun that transforms through poetry personal experience into collective. But the lyric you is under duress here, has been since childhood. "You smell good," a little white girl whom she allowed to copy her answers tells her. The lyric you that informs this poem is so vulnerable you wince and laugh along with her.

But it is also aspirational. *Don't Let Me Be Lonely* is the title of her last book. Her lyric you is a plea for both solidity and connection. Even at its most purely lyrical, there is an undercurrent of that yearning:

> Blue ceiling calling a body into the midst of azure, oceanic,
> as ocean blushes the blues it can't absorb, reflecting back a day
>
> the day frays, night, not night, this fright passes through
> the eye crashing into you, is this you?
>
> (p. 75)

The lyric you, changing on the page, and behind it the fragile "I," the useful myth of a unified self (Bromberg, 1998):

> Sometimes "I" is supposed to hold what is not there until it is. Then
> *what is* comes apart the closer you are to it.
> This makes the first person a symbol for something
> The pronoun barely holding the person together.
>
> (p. 70)

The indictment

Part documentary, *Citizen* indicts racism everywhere, from the police-gun streets of St. Louis or Baltimore to the mother who offers to sit in the middle seat so her daughter won't have to sit by a black person to the chair judge calling Serena Williams for a fake toe-fault on the white-lined courts of the U.S. Open.

Part II of the book features a long retrospective essay on Serena Williams. Watching sports is the great escape, but Rankine shuts the sound off to be spared the racist comments. Meanwhile, the reader may be tempted to ask, what's up with this in the middle of a poem? But keep reading. In 2004, the chair judge, Mariana Alves, essentially throws the U.S. Open to Jennifer Capriati. "Though no one was saying anything explicitly about Serena's black body, you are not the only viewer who thought it was getting in the way of Alves's sight line," she writes (p. 27). In 2009, 2011: more of the same. Then in 2012, a final image, a white tennis player, former champion, stuffing towels in her bra and backside to imitate Williams's shape. No respite, Rankine seems to be saying, even in my living room, watching my favorite sport, my favorite player.

And then we move closer to actual documentary, with a series of soundtrack-like "situation videos" of racial injustices and murders, created in collaboration with John Lucas, her filmmaker husband. Some familiar: Hurricane Katrina, Trayvon Martin; some new to this reader, such as James Craig Anderson, a 49-year-old black man run down by a white teenager in a pickup truck in Mississippi. With a dig at William Carlos Williams ("The pure products of America/go crazy"), Rankine writes,

> Then the pickup truck is beating the black object to the ground and the tire marks crushed organs. Then the audio, I ran that nigger over, is itself a record-breaking hot June day in the twenty-first century.
>
> The pickup returns us to live cruelty, like sunrise, red streaks falling from dawn to asphalt – then again this pickup is not about beauty. It is a pure product.
>
> (p. 94)

"An American Lyric"

Ezra Pound (1968) defined the epic in the broadest possible terms as a poem that contains history. The writers who had an eye toward history that we have discussed in this book – Virgil, Dante, Blake, Whitman, Milosz and perhaps Celan – have described in their own ways how the self either makes history or is carried along by its currents. They have also, at times, described the way the self tries to rise above or even oppose those currents. The former usually take the form of narratives or epics, the latter of lyrics. Blake, unique among them, combined both impulses as he described history taking place *inside* the self, thus forever linking inner transformation with outer revolution.

Citizen, self-identified as "An American Lyric," is a special case here as well, for it is a poem of the self in struggle with history – or at least with the dark history of American racism – trying, in its own quiet way, to change it. But it is also and most profoundly a search for identity, for individual survival in a racist world. Even at its most documentary, decrying this lynching, that innocent-seeming slight, the poem makes a deep connection to the author's subjective experience. And this, we come to see, is its point. Our selves, our bodies, and lives are drenched with history.

"Piper sit thee down and write/in a book that all may read," Blake writes in the introduction to the *Songs* (1970, p. 7). A simple act of poetic invention that sets in motion the progression of consciousness from Innocence to Experience and hopefully to Higher Innocence. *Citizen* is clearly a Song of Experience, but its very existence, its shifting voice, its radical formal inventiveness, points toward a new possibility:

> Stand where you are.
> You begin to move around in search of the steps it will
> take before you are thrown back into your own body back
> into your own need to be found.

> (p. 70)

The verb "thrown" suggests for me Heidegger's concept of "thrownness," our being, in Simon Critchley's words, "delivered over to the world" (2005, p. 30). Against all the assaults on the black body that Rankine documents, she here asserts her thrownness into that body, into her human situation, her need to be found. Her example shines a ray of hope for black people. And discourages white people from using a fantasy of white privilege as a defense against their own thrownness.

Case vignette

Ray is my longest-tenured client, but we almost didn't make it past our first year. He came to me as a recovering addict, needing an outpatient therapist to facilitate his transfer from a residential program. Ray had used dope to medicate away his shame, shame at growing up with a mother who had serial relationships and serial families, shame at being a sensitive boy on the brutal West Oakland streets. But this sensitivity is what I liked in Ray. Vividly describing his various counselors and fellow addicts, he cut through people's ruses. (This sensitivity eventually served him well in his long career as a residential treatment counselor for youth.) I was flattered that he saw something in me and wanted right away for us to work together. His recovery, his new self, was young, though. He referred to himself as "starving at the Safeway"; there was food and nourishment everywhere, but he didn't know how to take it.

One day, he came to me genuinely excited. He'd found a new path. He'd met a minister of the Black Muslims, a follower of Louis Farrakhan. The man had told him the truth about black history, including the truth about how black people were sold into slavery by the Jews, how the Jews owned all the slave ships and most of the slaves. I tried to keep my emotions under control, but very soon I lost it completely.

"That is absolute bullshit," I shouted. "There weren't enough Jews around back then in England or America to account for the slave trade. That's just a bunch of anti-Semitic nonsense they're feeding you." By the end of my outburst, I was shaking, and Ray was completely shaken. I was surprised that he came back again, but he did. "You went absolutely crazy on me," he opened. "I didn't even know you were Jewish," he kept saying. "How was I to know you were Jewish?"

"It wasn't your doing at all," I replied. "You don't owe me any apology. There's a part of me you hit accidentally that *is* completely crazy, that thinks about what my people went through in the Holocaust, and just loses it. You didn't deserve that. Your people have done nothing to my people. You just struck a nerve, and I reacted."

"I have that part too," Ray replied. "It's part of the reason I used dope. It makes me not feel so bad about myself, knowing how you can lose it so bad too, and still keep going."

It was a moment of meeting of sorts, where black and white, victim and victimizer, were oscillating out of their orbits. A whole system of roles and histories thrown up in the air like the child's card game of 52 pick-up. I don't know if Ray and I would ever have learned to know and love each other as deeply as we do if I hadn't met him in his darkness; if I hadn't let him put me back together.

Citizen does something similar for the reader. Rankine is a great artist. She never loses her poetic control. But she does grant us access to the shatterings, little and grand, that have struck her to the core, and she lets us inside the process of her reassembly.

References

Aron, L., and Starr, K. (2013). *A Psychotherapy for the People*. New York and London: Routledge.

Atwood, G. (1997). Comment made at Meet the Author's session. *20th Conference on the Psychology of the Self*, Chicago, IL, November 15, 1997.

Atwood, G., and Stolorow, R. (1984). *Structures of Subjectivity*. Hillsdale, NJ: The Analytic Press.

Barrows, A. (2016). *We Are the Hunger*. Hemet, CA: Kelsey Books.

Beebe, B., Cohen, P., and Lachmann, F. (2016). *The Mother-Infant Interaction Picture Book*. New York: Norton.

Beebe, B., and Lachmann, F. (1992). The contribution of mother-infant mutual influence to the origin of self and object representations. In N. Skolnick and S. Warshaw (Eds.), *Relational Perspectives in Psychoanalysis*. Hillsdale, NJ: The Analytic Press.

Beebe, B., and Lachmann, F. (2002). *Infant Research and Adult Treatment*. Hillsdale, NJ: The Analytic Press.

Beebe, B., and Lachmann, F. (2014). *The Origins of Attachment: Infant Research and Adult Treatment*. New York and London: Routledge.

Beebe, B., and McRorie, T. (1996). A model for love in the 21st century: Infant research, literature, romantic attachment, and psychoanalysis. Presented at the *19th Annual Conference on the Psychology of the Self*, Washington, DC.

Bion, W. (1965). *Transformations*. London: Heinemann.

Blake, W. (1970). *The Complete Poetry and Prose of William Blake*, S.F. Damon, Ed. New York: Doubleday.

Bloch, C. (2015). *Swimming in the Rain*. Pittsburgh, PA: Autumn House.

Boland, E. (2008). *New Collected Poems*. New York: Norton.

Bollas, C. (1987). *The Shadow of the Object*. London: Free Association Press.

Boston Change Process Group. (2010). *Change in Psychotherapy*. New York: Norton.

Brandchaft, B., Doctors, S., and Sorter D. (2010). *Toward an Emancipatory Psychoanalysis*. New York and London: Routledge.

Bromberg, P. (1998). *Standing in the Spaces*. New York: Psychology Press.

Celan, P. (1986). *Last Poems*, K. Washburn and M. Guilleman, Trans. San Francisco, CA: North Point.

Coates, T.-N. (2015). *Between the World and Me*. New York: Random House.

Coburn, W.J. (2014). *Psychoanalytic Complexity*. London and New York: Routledge.

Constantine, P. et al., ed. (2010) *The Greek Poets*. New York and London: Norton.

Critchley, S. (2005). *Things Merely Are*. New York and London: Routledge.

Damon, S.F. (1979). *A Blake Dictionary*. Boulder, CO: Shambala Press.

Dante, A. (1961). *The Purgatorio*, J. Ciardi, Trans. New York: Mentor.

Dante, A. (1969). *La Vita Nuova*, B. Reynolds, Trans. New York: Penguin.

Dante, A. (2002). *Inferno*, M. Palma, Trans. New York: Norton.

Dickinson, E. (1960). *The Complete Poems of Emily Dickinson*, T. Johnson, Ed. New York: Little Brown.

Duncan, R. (1960). Often I am permitted to return to a meadow. In *The Opening of the Field*. New York: Grove Press.

Duncan, R. (1968a). *The Truth and Life of Myth*. Fremont, MI: The Sumac Press.

Duncan, R. (1968b). *Bending the Bow*. New York: New Directions.

Ekman, P. (2003). *Emotions Revealed*. New York: Holt.

Emerson, R.W. (2003). An address to the Divinity School at Harvard. In B. Atkinson (Ed.), *Selected Writings of Ralph Waldo Emerson*. New York: Signet Classics.

Euripedes (2005). *Medea*, Ian Johnson, Trans. Nanaimo, BC, Canada: Prideaux Street Publications.

Fonagy, P. et al. (2002). *Affect Regulation, Mentalization and the Development of the Self*. New York: Other Press.

Forché, C. (1993). Introduction. In C. Forché (Ed.), *Against Forgetting*. New York: Norton.

Fosha, D. (2000). *The Transforming Power of Affect*. New York: Basic.

Freud, S. (1908 [1950]). *Creative Writers and Day Dreaming*, Standard Edition, Vol. 9. London: Hogarth Press, pp. 143–153.

Freud, S. (1981). *The Interpretation of Dreams*. Standard Edition, Vol. 5. London: Hogarth Press.

Frye, N. (1990a). *Words With Power*. New York: Harcourt, Brace, Jovanovich.

Frye, N. (1990b). *Fearful Symmetry*. Princeton, NJ: Princeton University Press.

George, C., Kaplan, N., and Main, M. (1985). The Adult Attachment Interview. Unpublished manuscript, University of California at Berkeley, Berkeley.

Gerson, S. (2009). When the third is dead: Memory, mourning, and witnessing in the aftermath of the Holocaust. *The International Journal of Psychoanalysis*, 90: 1341–1357.

Gleckner, R. (1966). Point of view and context in Blake's Songs. In N. Frye (Ed.), *Blake: A Collection of Critical Essays*. Edgewood Cliffs, NJ: Prentice Hall.

Graham, J. (1995). *The Dream of the Unified Field*. New York: Ecco.

Greenberg, J. (1991). *Oedipus and Beyond*. Cambridge, MA: Harvard University Press.

Hagman, G. (2005). *Aesthetic Experience: Beauty, Creativity and the Search for the Ideal*. New York: Rodopi Press.

Hagman, G. (2015). *Art, Creativity and Psychoanalysis*. New York: Routledge.

Hass, R. (1984). *Twentieth Century Pleasures*. New York: Ecco Press.

Hass, R. (2017). *A Little Book on Form*. New York: Ecco.

Heaney, S. (1995). *The Redress of Poetry*. New York: Farrar, Strauss & Giroux.

Heaney, S. (2016). Introduction. In S. Heaney (Trans.), *The Aeneid Book VI*. New York: Farrar, Strauss and Giroux.

Homer. (1990). *The Iliad*, Robert Fagles, Trans. New York: Viking.

Howe, S. (1985). *My Emily Dickinson*. New York: New Directions.

Jaffe, J., Beebe, B., Feldstein, S., Crown, C., and Jasnow, M. (2001). Rhythms of dialogue in infancy. *Monograph Series of the Society for Research in Child Development, No. 264*, 66(2).

James, W. (1920). *The Varieties of Religious Experience*. New York: Longmans and Green and Co.

Keats, J. (1959). Letter to George and Thomas Keats. In Douglas Bush (Ed.), *Selected Poems and Letters*. Cambridge: Houghton Mifflin.

Knoblauch, S. (2000). *The Musical Edge of Therapeutic Dialogue*. Hillsdale, NJ: The Analytic Press.

Kohut, H. (1959). Introspection, empathy, and psychoanalysis: An examination of the relation between mode of observation and theory. In P.H. Ornstein (Ed.), *The Search for the Self*, Vol. 1. New York: International Universities Press.

Kohut, H. (1966). Forms and transformations of narcissism. *Journal of the American Psychoanalytic Association*, 14: 243–272.

Kohut, H. (1971). *The Analysis of the Self*. New York: International Universities Press.

Kohut, H. (1977). *The Restoration of the Self*. New York: International Universities Press.

Kohut, H. (1984). *How Does Analysis Cure?* Chicago, IL: University of Chicago Press.

Kohut, H. (1985). Creativeness, charisma, group psychology. In C. Strozier (Ed.), *Kohut and the Humanities*. New York: Norton, pp. 171–211.

Lacan, J. (1991). *Seminars of Jacques Lacan Book II*. Cambridge: Cambridge University Press.

Lehman, D. (1998). *The Last Avant Garde*. New York: Doubleday.

Levertov, D. (1991a). Poetry, prophecy and survival. In *Selected Essays*. New York: New Directions.

Levertov, D. (1991b). The poet in the world. In *Selected Essays*. New York: New Directions.

Levertov, D. (1992). Some notes on organic form. In *New and Selected Essays*. New York: New Directions, pp. 67–73.

Levertov, D. (2013). *The Collected Poems of Denise Levertov*. P. Lacey and A. Dewey (Eds.). New York: New Directions.

MacAllistar, A. (1961) Introduction. In Dante, A., *The Purgatorio*. J. Ciardi Trans. New York: Mentor.

Main, M., and Hesse, E. (1990). Parents' unresolved traumatic experiences are related to infant disorganized attachment status: Is frightened and/or frightening parental behavior the linking mechanism? In M.T. Greenberg, D. Cicchetti, and E.M. Cummings (Eds.), *Attachment in the Preschool Years: Theory, Research and Intervention*. Chicago, IL: University of Chicago Press, pp. 161–182.

Marcuse, H. (1955). *Eros and Civilization*. Boston: Beacon Press.

McGuire, D. (2017). *American Dream with Exit Wound*. San Francisco, CA: IF SF Publishing.

Meerloo, J. (1968). The universal language of rhythm. In J. Leedy (Ed.), *Poetry Therapy*. Philadelphia, PA: Lippincott, pp. 52–66.

Milosz, C. (1981). *Nobel Lecture*. New York: Farrar Strauss and Giroux.

Milosz, C. (2001). *New and Collected Poems*. New York: Ecco.

Mitchell, S. (1993). *Hope and Dread in Psychoanalysis*. New York: Basic Books.

Mitchell, S. (1995). *Hope and Dread in Psychoanalysis*. New York: Basic Books.

Ogden, T. (1995). *Subjects of Analysis*. Northvale, NJ: Jason Aronson.

Ogden, T. (2004). The analytic third: Implications for psychoanalytic theory and technique. *The Psychoanalytic Quarterly*, 72: 167–196.

Olds, S. (2012). The clasp. In *Strike Sparks: Selected Poems 1980–2002*. New York: Knopf.

Oppen, G. (2002). Sarah in her father's arms. In *New Collected Poems*. New York: New Directions, p. 51.

Orange, D. (2010). *Thinking for Clinicians*. New York and London: Routledge.

Orange, D., Atwood, G., and Stolorow, R. (1997). *Working Intersubjectivity*. Hillsdale, NJ: The Analytic Press.

Petrarch, F. (1981). *Songs and Sonnets*, N. Kilmer, Trans. San Francisco, CA: North Point Press.

Pound, E. (1968). How to read. In *The Literary Essays of Ezra Pound*. New York: New Directions.

Rankine, C. (2004). *Don't Let Me Be Lonely*. Minneapolis, MN: Graywolf.

Rankine, C. (2014). *Citizen*. Minneapolis, MN: Graywolf.

Rappoport, E. (2015). Dynamic linking of psyche and soma: Somatic experiencing and embodied mentalization. In J. Blessler and K. Starr (Eds.), *Relational Psychoanalysis and Psychotherapy Integration*. New York and London: Routledge, pp. 136–158.

Reik, T. (1968). ne t'es-tu fias mal, mon enfant. In J. Leedy (Ed.), *Poetry Therapy*. Philadelphia, PA: Lippincott, pp. 5–7.

Rich, A. (1993). *What Is Found There*. New York: Norton.

Ringstrom, P.A. (2001). Cultivating the improvisational in psychoanalytic treatment. *Psychoanalytic Dialogues*, 1(5): 727–754.

Sachs, H. (1942). *The Creative Unconscious: Studies in the Psycho-Analysis of Art*. Cambridge, MA: Sci-Art Publishers.

Schwartz, J. (2017). Coming into being as an artist and psychotherapist: Keeping self from falling together too soon. In G. Hagman (Ed.), *Art, Creativity and Psychoanalysis*. New York and London: Routledge, pp. 1–19.

Science Daily. (2017). Boosting natural brain opioids may be a better way to treat anxiety, research shows. www.sciencedaily.com/releases/2017/03/170323105829.htm

Scott, P.D. (2017). *Ecstatic Pessimist: Czeslaw Milosz as a Poet of Catastrophe and Hope*. Unpublished manuscript.

Shaddock, D. (1997). *Empty, after Blake 7*. Ruah VII, p. 44.

Shaddock, D. (1998). *From Impasse to Intimacy*. Northvale, NJ: Jason Aronson.

Shaddock, D. (2000). *Contexts and Connections*. New York: Basic Books.

Shaddock, D. (2010). The opening of the field: Thoughts on the poetics of psychoanalytic treatment. *Psychoanalytic Inquiry*, 30: 243–253.

Shaddock, D. (2012). Asymptote. *IJPSP*, 7(4): 559.

Shaddock, D. (2013). The sudden angel affrighted me. *Tikkun*, 28(1): 52–58.

Slavin, M., and Kriegman, D. (1992). *The Adaptive Design of the Human Psyche*. New York: Guilford.

Southwell, R. (1963). The Burning Babe. In W. Taylor and D. Hall (Eds.), *Poetry in English*. New York: Macmillan.

Stern, D. (1985). *The Interpersonal World of the Infant*. New York: Basic Books.

Stern, D. (1995). *The Motherhood Constellation*. London: Karnac.

Stern, D., Sander, W., Nahum, J., Harrison, A., Lyons-Ruth, K., Morgan, A., Bruschweiler-Stern, N., and Tronick, E. (1998). Non-interpretive methods in psychoanalytic psychotherapy: The something more than interpretation. *The International Journal of Psychoanalysis*, 79: 903–922.

Stern, S. (2017). *Needed Relationships and Psychoanalytic Healing*. New York: Routledge.

Stevens, W. (1978). *The Collected Poems of Wallace Stevens*. New York: Knopf.

Stevens, W. (1982). *Opus Posthumous*, W.M. French, Ed. New York: Vintage.

Stolorow, R. (1993). Thoughts on the nature of therapeutic action of psychoanalytic interpretation. In A. Goldberg (Ed.), *The Widening Scope of Self Psychology, Progress in Self Psychology*, Vol. 9. Hillsdale, NJ: The Analytic Press, pp. 31–94.

Stolorow, R. (1997). Dynamic, dyadic, intersubjective systems: An evolving paradigm for psychoanalysis. *Psychoanalytic Psychology*, 14(3): 337.

Stolorow, R. (2007). *Trauma and Human Existence*. New York: Routledge.

Stolorow, R. (2012). What did we learn from 9/11? *Psychology Today*, blog post. www.psychologytoday.com/blog/feeling-relating-existing/201209/what-did-we-learn-911

Stolorow, R., and Atwood, G. (1992). *Contexts of Being*. Hillsdale, NJ: The Analytic Press.

Stolorow, R., Atwood, G., and Orange, D. (2002). *Worlds of Experience*. Hillsdale, NJ: Analytic Press.

Stolorow, R., Brandchaft, B., and Atwood, G. (1987). *Psychoanalytic Treatment: An Intersubjective Approach*. Hillsdale, NJ: The Analytic Press.

Thelan, E., and Smith, L. (1994). *A Dynamic Systems Approach to the Development of Cognition and Action*. Cambridge, MA: MIT Press.

Tolpin, M. (2002). Doing psychoanalysis of normal development: Forward edge transferences. *Progress in Self Psychology*, 18: 167–190.

Vandler, H. (1986). *Words Chosen Out of Desire*. Cambridge, MA: Harvard University Press.

Virgil. (2006). *The Aeneid*, R. Fagles, Trans. New York: Viking.

Virgil. (2016). *The Aeneid Book VI*, S. Heaney, Trans. New York: Farrar, Straus Giroux.

Wagner, L. (1976). Introduction to *Interviews with William Carlos Williams*. Linda Wagner, ed. New York: New Directions.

Washburn, K. (1986). Introduction. In K. Washburn and M. Guillamin (Trans.), *Paul Celan Last Poems*. San Francisco, CA: North Point.

Whitman, W. (1910). *Democratic Vistas*. Iowa City, Iowa: The University of Iowa Press.

Whitman, W. (1983). *Leaves of Grass: The 1892 Edition*. New York: Bantam.

Williams, W.C. (1962). Asphodel that Greeny Flower. In *Pictures from Brueghel and Other Poems*. New York: New Directions.

Williams, W.C. (1963). *Paterson*. New York: New Directions.

Williams, W.C. (1967). *The Autobiography of William Carlos Williams*. New York: New Directions.

Williams, W.C. (1976). *Interviews with William Carlos Williams*, Linda Wagner, Ed. New York: New Directions.

Williams, W.C. (1991a). *The Collected Poems of William Carlos Williams, Volume I: 1909–1939*, A. Walton Litz and Christopher MacGowan, Eds. New York: New Directions.

Williams, W.C. (1991b). *The Collected Later Poems of William Carlos Williams*, Christopher MacGowan, Ed. New York: New Directions.

Winnicott, D.W. (1965). Ego distortions in terms of true and false self. In D. Winnicott (Ed.), *The Maturational Process and the Facilitating Environment*. New York: International Universities Press.

Winnicott, D.W. (1971a). Transitional objects and transitional phenomena. In *Playing and Reality*. New York and London: Routledge, pp. 1–25.

Winnicott, D.W. (1971b). *Playing and Reality*. Hove, UK: Psychology Press.

Winnicott, D.W. (1984 [1956]). Primary maternal preoccupation. In D.W. Winnicott (Ed.), *Through Paediatrics to Psychoanalysis: Collected Papers*. London: Karnac, pp. 300–305.

Winnicott, D.W. (2016). *The Collected Works of D. W. Winnicott: Volume 6, 1960–1963*. Lesley Caldwell and Helen Taylor Robinson, Ed. Oxford: Oxford University Press. https://doi.org/1093/med:psych/9780190271381.001.0001

Wordsworth, W. (2004). *Selected Poems*, S. Gill, Ed. New York: Penguin.

Yeats, W.B. (1996). *The Collected Poetry of William Butler Yeats*. R. Finneran, Ed. New York: Scribner.

Index